A BIRDER'S GUIDE
TO
NEW HAMPSHIRE

A BIRDER'S GUIDE TO NEW HAMPSHIRE

by

Alan Delorey

American Birding Association

Library of Congress Catalog Number: 95-81410

ISBN Number: 1-878788-11-6

First Edition

   1   2   3   4   5   6   7   8   9

Printed in the United States of America

Publisher

   American Birding Association, Inc.

   George G. Daniels, *Chair, ABA Publications Committee*

Series Editor

   Paul J. Baicich

Associate Editors

   Cindy Lippincott and Bob Berman

Copy Editor

   Hugh Willoughby

Layout, Typography, and Maps

   Cindy Lippincott and Bob Berman

      using CorelVENTURA, ver. 5.0 and CorelDRAW ver. 5.0

Photography

   front cover: *Spruce Grouse*, Charles H. Willey

   back cover: *Bicknell's Thrush*, Steven Faccio

      Purple Finch, Brian Small

   author photo: Barbara Delorey

   black-and-white photography: Alan Delorey

Illustrations

   Georges Dremeaux, Shawneen E. Finnegan, Barry W. Van Dusen

Distributed by

   American Birding Association Sales

   PO Box 6599

   Colorado Springs, Colorado 80934-6599 USA

   tel: (800) 634-7736; fax: (800) 590-2473

European and UK Distribution

   Subbuteo Natural History Books, Ltd.

   Treuddyn, Mold, Clwyd

      CH7 4LN UK tel: 0352-770581; fax: 0352-771590

Printed on recycled paper containing 50% recycled fiber with 15% post-consumer waste.

To my wife Barbara,

my favorite birding companion

American Birding Association Code of Ethics

We, the Membership of the American Birding Association, believe that all birders have an obligation at all times to protect wildlife, the natural environment, and the rights of others. We therefore pledge ourselves to provide leadership in meeting this obligation by adhering to the following general guidelines of good birding behavior.

I. Birders must always act in ways that do not endanger the welfare of birds or other wildlife.

In keeping with this principle, we will

- Observe and photograph birds without knowingly disturbing them in any significant way.
- Avoid chasing or repeatedly flushing birds.
- Only sparingly use recordings and similar methods of attracting birds and not use these methods in heavily birded areas.
- Keep an appropriate distance from nests and nesting colonies so as not to disturb them or expose them to danger.
- Refrain from handling birds or eggs unless engaged in recognized research activities.

II. Birders must always act in ways that do not harm the natural environment.

In keeping with this principle, we will

- Stay on existing roads, trails, and pathways whenever possible to avoid trampling or otherwise disturbing fragile habitat.
- Leave all habitat as we found it.

III. Birders must always respect the rights of others.

In keeping with this principle, we will

- Respect the privacy and property of others by observing "No Trespassing" signs and by asking permission to enter private or posted lands.
- Observe all laws and the rules and regulations which govern public use of birding areas.
- Practice common courtesy in our contacts with others. For example, we will limit our requests for information, and we will make them at reasonable hours of the day.
- Always behave in a manner that will enhance the image of the birding community in the eyes of the public.

IV. Birders in groups should assume special responsibilities.

As group members, we will

- Take special care to alleviate the problems and disturbances that are multiplied when more people are present.
- Act in consideration of the group's interest, as well as our own.
- Support by our actions the responsibility of the group leader(s) for the conduct of the group.

As group leaders, we will

- Assume responsibility for the conduct of the group.
- Learn and inform the group of any special rules, regulations, or conduct applicable to the area or habitat being visited.
- Limit groups to a size that does not threaten the environment or the peace and tranquility of others.
- Teach others birding ethics by our words and example.

TABLE OF CONTENTS

PREFACE

Doing the field research for this book has been very enjoyable. My wife, Barbara Delorey, and I have visited and explored every birding location—often during multiple seasons—presented in this book. In fact, we have birded most of the sites numerous times. During this field work, we recorded up to 250 species of birds per year in New Hampshire.

I had many splendid birding experiences while conducting the field work for this book. Some of my fondest memories include the Spruce Grouse, Boreal Chickadees, and Mourning Warblers at East Inlet; the Long-eared Owl, Cape May Warbler, and Clay-colored Sparrow on Star Island; the Acadian Flycatcher and Cerulean Warbler at Pawtuckaway State Park; the nesting Black-backed Woodpeckers in Jefferson Notch; the song of the Bicknell's Thrush on Cannon Mountain; the Pied-billed Grebe, Northern Pintail, Northern Shoveler, Canvasback, and American Coots on Powder House Pond in Exeter; the Harlequin Duck and Barrow's Goldeneye wintering along the coast; and the King Eider off Odiorne Point. Seabrook Harbor provided 24 Whimbrels in late July and 9 Hudsonian Godwits in August. The Snowy Owl perched on the bathhouse at Hampton Beach State Park was so easy to photograph. Nothing among bird sounds compares to the *glunk-ga-glunk* of the American Bittern at Cascade Marsh on a spring evening. The Buff-breasted and Baird's Sandpipers on North Hampton State Beach almost posed to have their pictures taken. Three Pectoral Sandpipers and a Wilson's Phalarope cooperated by snuggling together to be photographed in Hampton Falls Marsh.

Once you have experienced New Hampshire, I am sure that you will agree with me. The state is a wonderful place for birding and for exploring nature.

Alan Delorey
October 1995

ACKNOWLEDGEMENTS

Writing this book has been both a great pleasure and a learning experience. I would like to thank the following people for their assistance. Ann Comer reviewed my original manuscript for grammatical correctness. Dennis Abbott provided assistance with the bar-graphs, did a complete review of the manuscript, and offered advice throughout the project. Kimball Elkins shared his many years of New Hampshire birding experience by reviewing the manuscript. Not only did my wife, Barbara, accompany me on every birding exploration trip as we conducted the field work for this book, but she also reviewed the manuscript countless times.

Others who helped with field-checking and comments include Michelle D. Anderson, David Deifik, Terry McEneaney, and Richard K. Walton. The artists who provided the book's fine illustrations were Georges Dremeaux, Shawneen E. Finnegan, and Barry W. Van Dusen. The photographers of the cover photos were Steven Faccio, Brian Small, and Charles H. Willey.

The ABA editorial staff was indispensable to the birth and delivery of this book. Paul J. Baicich, the series editor, provided general guidance. Cindy Lippincott did the maps and assisted editorially. Bob Berman, another associate editor, also provided technical assistance. And not only did Hugh Willoughby do the copy editing, but he also helped to add important details to assist those unfamiliar with birding New Hampshire.

A work such as this is never complete. New discoveries are constantly being made about bird nesting and migratory preferences. Habitats change from both natural causes and human intervention (both helpful and harmful). These changes can have a direct influence on wildlife. While every attempt has been made to ensure accuracy as of the time this book was published, there are bound to be a few errors, and conditions are sure to change. I anticipate producing updated editions of this work in the years to come. If you have any comments or suggestions concerning this book, please write to me in care of the American Birding Association, P.O. Box 6599, Colorado Springs, Colorado 80934.

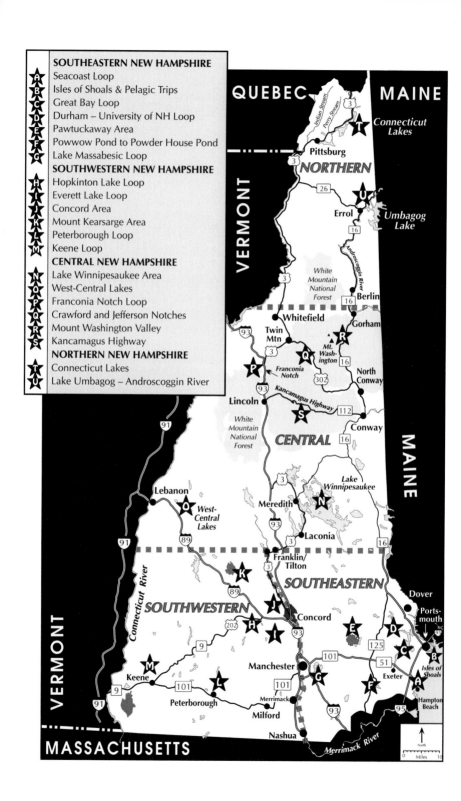

INTRODUCTION

This section of the book provides some general background information on New Hampshire: its history, geography, economy, weather, camping, and lodging—as well as how to make the best use of the book.

HISTORY

New Hampshire has a colorful history, stemming from its beginning as one of the thirteen original colonies. The first European colonization was an English settlement in 1623 at Odiorne Point at the mouth of the Piscataqua River, near present-day Portsmouth. Delegates from New Hampshire signed the Declaration of Independence and ratified the Constitution, becoming the critical ninth state to do so, thus activating the new Union on June 21, 1788. The state is named after the English county of Hampshire.

New Hampshire has several famous historical figures. General John Stark (1728-1822), a Revolutionary War general, led New Hampshire volunteers at the Battle of Bunker Hill, June 17, 1775. He also coined the state motto: "Live Free or Die," more than a mere license-plate decoration. Josiah Bartlett (1729-1795) was a Revolutionary War patriot who signed the Declaration of Independence for New Hampshire. Daniel Webster (1782-1851), the famous statesman, born near Franklin, New Hampshire, became a United States senator and secretary of state under Presidents Harrison and Fillmore. Franklin Pierce (1804-1869), the 14th president of the United States, had a homestead in the town of Hillsborough which can still be visited today.

The Robert Frost farm in Derry, New Hampshire, where the honored poet lived from 1900 to 1911, is a state historic site and is open to the public during the summer. Frost once wrote that his years on the Derry farm formed the core of all his writing. Daniel Chester French (1850-1931), a sculptor from New Hampshire, is probably best known for the Minute Man statue in Concord, Massachusetts, and the sculpture of President Lincoln in the Lincoln Memorial, Washington, D.C. In more modern times, America's first astronaut, Alan B. Shepard, Jr., was from Derry, New Hampshire, which was subsequently nicknamed "Space Town USA". Thornton Wilder's play *Our Town* and the novel *Peyton*

Place by Grace Metalious were both based on New Hampshire communities.

New Hampshire has a large number of Native American place-names. Notable tribes living in the area when European settlers first arrived were the Ossipee, Nashua, Penacook, Piscataqua, Squamscott, and Winnipesaukee. Many rivers, lakes, mountains, and other places throughout the state still bear the names given to them by these tribes.

Indeed, Dartmouth, one of the country's oldest and most prestigious colleges, founded in 1769, was originally chartered for the "education and instruction of the Youth of the Indian Tribes," rather than the education of "English Youth and others." Today, it is an educational center for medicine, engineering, and business administration, with a very prestigious cultural center.

On the ornithological scene, New Hampshire has its important history, too. When the United States was very young, Jeremy Belknap wrote the *History of New Hampshire* and listed some 130 bird species. Among other birds, it listed "Penguin *Alca impennis*" and "Wild Pigeon *Columba migratoria*," clearly referring to the now-extinct Great Auk and Passenger Pigeon. Other birds listed by Belknap in 1792 included "Boblincoln" (Bobolink), "Partridge" (Ruffed Grouse), "Quail" (Northern Bobwhite), and "Great Crested Woodpecker" (Pileated Woodpecker).

Sadly, from the time of Belknap's work to the mid-to-late 1800s, very little of importance was written to chronicle the birdlife of the state. This is particularly unfortunate, since such work might have followed land-use changes, from the ebb and flow of farm growth and abandonment, to the development of lumbering as a major factor in New Hampshire.

Elliot Coues (1842-1899) was born in New Hampshire. He did his initial birding as a youth near his home in Portsmouth, where his father was a shipowner. Before he was a teenager and had moved with his family to Washington, D.C., Coues had already taken notes on the birds in his area of New Hampshire. A founding member of the American Ornithologists' Union (AOU), Coues was to become one of the most influential ornithologists of his time, second perhaps only to Spencer F. Baird. His experiences combined those of a doctor, army officer, prolific writer, public speaker, exacting scientist, and mystic.

William Brewster (1851-1919), another founding member and a president of the AOU, spent several weeks each year over a period of 39 years (1871-1909) studying the birds of the Lake Umbagog region. Among other things, Brewster noted in his writings that the Passenger Pigeon was an abundant migrant and fairly common summer resident in the early 1870s around Lake Umbagog. Brewster also reported Golden

Eagles in the Umbagog region in the late 1800s, as probably nesting on nearby mountain cliffs. Brewster founded the Nuttall Ornithological Club of Cambridge, Massachusetts, in 1873. This was the first organization in the United States devoted to bird study; it is still very active today. Brewster was appointed the first curator of birds at the Harvard Museum of Comparative Zoology.

Several lists of the birds of New Hampshire were produced early in the 20th century. Glover M. Allen wrote *A List of the Birds of New Hampshire* in 1903, with 283 species mentioned. That same year, Ned Dearborn wrote *The Birds of Durham and Vicinity*, which included 252 species found within a twenty-mile radius of Durham, as part of a doctoral thesis. In 1911, Horace W. Wright's *The Birds of the Jefferson Region* listed 186 species. *A Preliminary List of Birds of Concord, New Hampshire* by F.B. White (a member of the Nuttall Ornithological Club) appeared in 1924.

New Hampshire also has an early history in bird clubs. In April of 1897, a group of about 30 women formed the New Hampshire Audubon Society. This organization quickly died out, leaving few records of its existence. The ideas of bird study and bird protection, however, were taking root.

Ernest Harold Baynes of Meriden began promoting the idea of bird protection in 1910, by collecting donations for bird houses and feeders. In December 1910, the Meriden Bird Club was organized in Meriden (a village in the town of Plainfield in west-central New Hampshire). In 1911 the club purchased a 32-acre farm for $1,000 to protect as a bird sanctuary. President Woodrow Wilson once visited the Meriden Sanctuary. A key factor in the success of the club, in a small New Hampshire town, was the presence of Kimball Union Academy, a secondary school for men and women. Both faculty and students supported the bird club with finances and labor. Much of their effort centered around setting up bird houses and feeders throughout the village and at the sanctuary. Soon these activities caused Meriden to become known as "the bird village." Such pioneer efforts prompted similar bird clubs to form in several other communities in New Hampshire and throughout the country in the early 1900s.

On February 26, 1914, the Audubon Society of New Hampshire (ASNH) chartered its existence at an organizational meeting in Nashua. The new fledgling Audubon Society conducted its first annual meeting on May 28, 1914, with 186 members. At the second annual meeting in 1915 there were 489 members, and by the third annual meeting in 1916 the ranks had swelled to 704 members. The society incorporated on June

29, 1920. ASNH published a checklist of the birds of New Hampshire in 1920 and published its first Quarterly Bulletin in 1921. To celebrate the 50th anniversary of ASNH, Roger Tory Peterson appeared as guest speaker at the annual meeting on June 27, 1964.

Today, the independent ASNH (not affiliated with the National Audubon Society) has several thousand members statewide. Its mission is to protect and conserve New Hampshire wildlife and habitat. There are several local chapters throughout the state which conduct birding trips. In particular, the Seacoast Chapter has an active field-trip program.

The ASNH also publishes a bird-oriented quarterly, *New Hampshire Bird Records*, available by subscription, and in the spring of 1995 published the *Atlas of Breeding Birds in New Hampshire*, edited by Carol R. Foss. (This project was co-sponsored by the ASNH, the University of New Hampshire, and the New Hampshire Fish and Game Department.) The ASNH cooperates in such worthwhile bird projects as the Peregrine Falcon Cliff Watch during the spring of each year, the Loon Preservation Committee, and the mid-winter Eagle Survey.

For more information on the organization, you can reach them as follows:

- Audubon Society of New Hampshire
  3 Silk Farm Road
  Concord, NH 03301
  603/224-9909

Some Geography and a Few Birds

What little flat land exists in New Hampshire is generally restricted to the seacoast region. Many visitors forget that New Hampshire actually has a seacoast. It even has islands—the Isles of Shoals. The seacoast is not large—only about 18 miles long—but its whole length is interesting for birders. It is almost all beach (with four state park beaches) with some rocky headlands and coves. Together with its accompanying harbors, bays, and marshes, the coastal area plays host to resident gulls, migrating shorebirds, and wintering waterfowl aplenty.

But New Hampshire is basically a state of rugged mountains and rolling hills. Many rivers, lakes, and ponds grace the state. There are some 1,300 natural lakes and ponds, plus five major rivers. New Hampshire extends 190 miles from Canada in the north to Massachusetts in the south. The Connecticut River defines the boundary with Vermont to the west. The state of Maine and the Atlantic Ocean make up the eastern boundary. New Hampshire has an area of about 9,000 square miles, ranking it the 44th state in size.

The character of New Hampshire today is that of a rural state. During the 18th and 19th centuries most of the state's forests were cleared for farming. This activity had a negative impact on the amount and variety of wildlife. However, during the 20th century, New Hampshire has been allowed to reforest. Today 85 percent of the state is covered by forests, making it one of the nation's most heavily forested states. There has also been a corresponding resurgence in wildlife, linked to the phasing-out of farms. (The shift, however, could also be characterized by a decrease in Northern Bobwhites, Ring-necked Pheasants, Eastern Meadowlarks, and grassland sparrows.)

The predominant type of forest in New Hampshire is characterized as Northern Hardwood. Typical species comprising this type of forest include Yellow, Gray, and Paper Birches, Sugar Maple, American Beech, Pin Cherry, Eastern Hemlock, and Red and White Pines. The northern tip of the state boasts a transition forest between Northern Hardwood and Boreal Forest. Typical species of Boreal Forest include White Spruce, Balsam Fir, Quaking Aspen, and Tamarack.

Pulling back from the seacoast region, one finds the southern lowlands, whose altitude ranges to about 1,100 feet, with a combination of evergreen and deciduous vegetation. This region has plenty of farmlands. But it is also the location of New Hampshire's urban and suburban development, with a good selection of the common yard and woodland birds. Combined, the seacoast and the southern lowland regions form the **Southeastern New Hampshire** portion of this book. Typical "backyard birds" of this area include Northern Mockingbird, Tufted Titmouse, Northern Cardinal, and House Finch, all successful arrivals and breeders within the last forty years. But the more interesting ones, those which occur more commonly here than elsewhere, are either coastally-bound (e.g., herons, gulls, and Seaside and Salt-marsh Sharp-tailed Sparrows) or associated with scattered woodlands (e.g., Yellow-billed Cuckoo, Fish Crow, White-eyed Vireo, and Orchard Oriole).

The second section of this book covers **Southwestern New Hampshire**. The southwest highlands are usually above 1,500 feet with a number of higher peaks and have modest spruce forests attractive to northern birds. Typical breeding passerine species of the southwest lowlands include Veery, Ovenbird, American Redstart, Blackburnian Warbler, White-throated Sparrow, and Dark-eyed Junco. Non-passerines include Turkey Vulture, Red-shouldered Hawk, Ruffed Grouse, and Wild Turkey.

The third geographical section of this book treats **Central New Hampshire**, covering the lakes region and the White Mountains. The lakes region, or the Winnipesaukee Lowlands, has less farmland and urban/suburban development than the southern lowlands. Therefore, it has more forests and, of course, lakes—including the dominant Lake Winnipesaukee. The altitude ranges usually between 500 and 1,200 feet, but reaches upward of 2,500 feet in the Ossipee Mountains. Characteristic breeding birds include Common Loon, Mallard, American Black Duck, Common Merganser, Red-eyed Vireo, American Redstart, Blackburnian Warbler, Ovenbird, and Chestnut-sided Warbler.

The White Mountains region dominates the north-central part of the state. This section includes one of New Hampshire's most prominent and famous features, Mount Washington in the Presidential Range of the White Mountains. Mount Washington is the highest point in the Northeast, rising to 6,288 feet above sea level. The White Mountain National Forest encompasses approximately 770,000 acres of the White Mountains, situated near the northern terminus of the Appalachians.

New Hampshire's nickname is "The Granite State". A trip through the White Mountains will convince you that the name fits. Granite structural remnants, especially stone walls, are common throughout the state. The famous "Old Man of the Mountain," a granite outcropping resembling a stoic human face, broods over Franconia Notch.

The highest peaks of the White Mountains introduce the Alpine Tundra habitat. As the elevation increases, the Northern Hardwood forest gives way to Boreal Forest, and finally at about 4,800 feet (the timberline) you enter the Alpine habitat. The divergent habitats introduced by increasing altitude directly affect what bird species are present. For example, Hermit Thrush ranges up to 3,000 feet, Swainson's Thrush is usually found from 1,500 to 4,500 feet, and Bicknell's Thrush typically nests above 3,000 feet and often near the timberline. Other typical birds of the White Mountains are broken down by altitudinal zone, and are described in the introduction to Chapter 3 of this book.

Northern New Hampshire is the final area covered in this book. The north country in the Connecticut Lakes area is home to extensive boggy boreal forests and numerous lakes and ponds. The well-known Lake Umbagog is in this region. Characteristic breeding birds of this area include Common Loon, Mallard, American Black Duck, Wood Duck, Yellow-bellied Flycatcher, Red-breasted Nuthatch, Bay-breasted Warbler, Magnolia Warbler, and Rusty Blackbird.

ECONOMY

The majority of New Hampshire's one million residents live in the southern portion of the state, where most of the cities and large towns are located. Although Concord is the state capital, Manchester is the largest city, followed closely by Nashua.

New Hampshire's most important industrial products are electrical and computer equipment, machinery, paper, and leather products. Agriculture still figures heavily in the state's economy with dairy farming, poultry farms, and apple orchards. About 75,000 gallons of maple syrup are produced annually. New England is famous for its seafood, especially lobster. Lobstering and fishing are small commercial industries in the state. *Yankee Magazine* and *The Old Farmer's Almanac* are produced in Dublin, New Hampshire. Tourism is a major industry with over one million visitors per year.

Some of the outdoor attractions in New Hampshire include alpine and cross-country skiing, camping, hiking, boating, fishing, fall foliage, and numerous scenic features in the White Mountains. For fall foliage enthusiasts there is even a toll-free "Fall Foliage Report" (800/258-3608) during September and October.

Popular tourist attractions in the state include the Conway Scenic Railroad in North Conway, a number of amusement parks for children, numerous golf courses, and, of course, many historic homes and sites throughout the state.

Moose are a popular tourist attraction in New Hampshire.

WEATHER

New Hampshire's Mount Washington, standing out high above other mountain peaks, claims the distinction of being "the home of the world's worst weather". This claim is based partially on the fact that Mount Washington boasts the highest wind velocity ever recorded on Earth. In 1934 the weather observatory on Mount Washington recorded a gust of 231 miles per hour. Fortunately, most of the state's weather is not that ferocious, and visitors should find birding in New Hampshire to be quite comfortable. Nevertheless, the winter birders here *must* have excellent cold-weather clothing.

The following table presents the average low and high temperatures (in degrees Fahrenheit) plus average precipitation (in inches of rain) for Concord, New Hampshire, during each month of the year.

	Jan	Feb	Mar	Apr	May	Jun	Jul	Aug	Sep	Oct	Nov	Dec
Low (F):	11	12	22	32	42	51	56	54	46	36	27	15
High (F):	32	34	42	56	69	78	83	81	72	62	48	35
Rain (in.):	3.1	2.8	3.3	3.3	3.5	3.5	3.6	3.6	3.5	3.6	4.0	3.8

BIRDS AND BIRDING

New Hampshire's official state bird is the Purple Finch. Care must be taken not to confuse this species with the now much more numerous House Finch, which was introduced to the East Coast in the 1940s, was first documented in New Hampshire in 1967, and has experienced a population explosion since then. The Purple Finch is pictured on the back cover of this book; the species is a more stocky, robust bird than the House Finch. The male is also more colorful, being a bright raspberry. The male House Finch is really red or orange/red (as opposed to raspberry) and has much more brown above. The male Purple Finch's sides and belly go from raspberry to white with none of the brown streaking found on the flanks of the House Finch. The females of the two species are easier to differentiate. Look for the more distinct ear-patch, whitish eyebrow, and cheek stripe in the female Purple Finch.

There are 342 bird species listed in the bar-graphs; 320 species are mentioned within the text at specific birding locations. The remaining 22 species are either the over-abundant ones, such as House Sparrows and European Starlings, or the rare and erratic ones, such that a precise location cannot be given. There are 70 permanent resident nesting species, 116 summer resident nesting species, 13 summer resident non-nesting species, 42 winter resident species, 53 migrants (within normal range), and 48 vagrants (outside normal range).

The Audubon Society of New Hampshire maintains a rare bird alert which operates from 603/224-9900.

The American Birding Association's *Membership Directory: ABA Birders* lists a few dozen New Hampshire residents who are members willing to assist visiting birders. To join the organization and obtain this publication contact:

- American Birding Association
  P.O. Box 6599
  Colorado Springs, CO 80934-6599
  800/850-2473

Another way to get the most out of birding information in New Hampshire is through CB-birding. The Brookline Bird Club (of Massachusetts) has set the standard in New England for the use of Citizens Band radio and birding. If you monitor CB Channel 25 while birding in New Hampshire, you may be able to contact other birders in the field and exchange up-to-the-minute birding tips. (The author's CB handle is "Bird-mobile.")

HOW TO USE THIS BOOK

This guide divides the state into four regions: southeastern, southwestern, central, and northern. For the purposes of this book, the southeastern and southwestern regions are south of the Tilton and Franklin areas and are basically separated by Interstate 93 (the major north-south highway in the state). The central area spans the state from Vermont to Maine, starting in the Tilton/Franklin area and going north through the White Mountains. The northern region contains all of the state north of the White Mountains to the Canadian border. These regions are shown on the map on the inside back cover of this book.

Within each region, birding locations are collected into trips, usually loops. Following these loops should help to organize your birding expeditions. A suggested length of time is listed for each trip. Directions are given, mile by mile, to lead you from one location to the next as you proceed through the loop.

Some of these trips can be enhanced by the use of a small boat; these cases are detailed in the text. (See "canoe trips" in Index.) In this regard, this book is unlike most other birdfinding guides. Using a rowboat, canoe, or kayak can truly open up new territory and increase your birding pleasure. Be sure to take along a life-jacket, bailing-can, spare paddle, and small anchor. (For regulations and a list of safety equipment required on boats, pick up a pamphlet at any boat store or marina.) You'll probably develop your own technique for birding afloat, poking your canoe or kayak into feeder streams and creeks, and using overhanging vegetation as a screen to create an impromptu blind. Drifting along while doing casual birding is also a pleasant technique.

The maps included in the book do not attempt to show every road and street. To keep the maps simple, clear, and easy to read, we show only major roads and landmarks, or those that are specifically referred to in the text. To see a "bigger picture" of the state and to find the starting-points for birding trips, a state road map or atlas is useful. (I have found the DeLorme atlas and gazetteer highly detailed and very helpful. Look for the 1995 edition; it is easier to read than the 1988 edition.)

The bird lists within the site descriptions are not meant to be exhaustive. Rather, they are intended to provide an example of what types of birds you may expect at each location. These lists also indicate the best places to locate difficult-to-find species.

There is a short section after the site-guides on the identification, status, and breeding biology of Bicknell's Thrush in New Hampshire. Many birders may be unfamiliar with this "new" species, and that part of the book should serve as a quick summary.

This book also includes bar-graph representations of the birds of New Hampshire through the year. These are designed to indicate the probability of seeing specific birds at the right time of year and in the right habitat.

SOME HAZARDS AFIELD

Both Dog Ticks (also called Wood Ticks) and Deer Ticks are found in New Hampshire, mainly in the southeastern section. The most prevalent is the common Dog Tick. However, the Deer Tick does occur and can carry Lyme disease. There have been a few dozen documented cases of it in the state. Ticks can be a problem from spring through fall, but May and June are probably the most troublesome months. The best way to prevent ticks is to avoid areas of brush and unmowed grass. If you are walking in areas of tall grass or are "bushwhacking," you should tuck your pant legs into your socks to prevent any ticks from crawling up inside your pant legs. If you wear light-colored clothing, you can more easily detect any little dark ticks that attach to your clothing. Spraying your socks and pant legs with a *DEET*-based spray may help to deter ticks. Using a spray with *Permethrin* on clothing (not on skin) has proven to be very effective, also.

During May you will encounter Black Flies. Throughout the summer mosquitoes are active. These pests are not usually a serious problem in New Hampshire; however, you may want to use an insect repellent to dissuade them. Another hazard to watch for is Poison Ivy, which is abundant throughout New Hampshire, except in the far-northern sections. It occurs as a low plant or as a climbing vine. You can recognize it by its clusters of three pointed, shiny green or sometimes reddish leaflets. If your skin comes into contact with Poison Ivy, wash with soap the affected area immediately to remove the oil residue that causes itching.

The opportunity to see a Black Bear or a Moose can be exciting for birders in the field, but caution should be exercised. Black Bears are active in large parts of New Hampshire. You are most likely to encounter one if you are hiking or camping. When camping, your food supply could attract Black Bears, so pay special attention to food storage and garbage disposal. If you see a Black Bear, remember that it is a wild animal and should be treated with caution and respect. *Never feed, touch, tease, or disturb any Black Bear.* Moose are also found in the state, and yellow "Caution—Moose Crossing" signs are seen along many a highway. There is, of course, the story of one local New Hampshire newspaper explaining an encounter between a Volkswagen and a Moose: "Rabbit Kills Moose," the headline read. These events, however, are no joke; moose/car collisions can be deadly—for both the car occupants and the Moose. The average Moose weighs an impressive 1,000 pounds and is six feet high at the shoulder. Most Moose are active at dusk and at night, particularly from May to October. Their eyes are set higher than car headlights, so they are not well-reflected; their dark legs and bodies camouflage them very well at night.

Finally, prepare for the weather conditions. Especially make appropriate preparations when going into the field in winter, when at times the weather can be bitterly cold. And at any time of year—even in mid-summer—pay particular attention to the weather when hiking in the mountains. There, dangerously severe weather can develop rapidly. Many ill-prepared hikers have died on Mount Washington, for example. Also, in the hottest months, many days can be both hot *and* humid, so bring plenty of fluids on your hikes at those times especially.

PRIVATE PROPERTY AND ETHICS

An estimated 20 percent of the state's six million acres are set aside from development. These include the White Mountain National Forest's 770,000 acres (about two-thirds of the state's protected land) and several state parks of some consequence. Some of the remaining protected acreage has been given to or purchased by conservation organizations—or is privately owned, but protected by conservation easements.

Moreover, large tracts of land are owned by paper and timber companies (e.g., in the Connecticut Lakes region, about 75 percent of the land belongs to Champion International Corporation). Under the present open-land policy, these properties are open for public day-use (no camping or fires) at no charge, but their primary purpose is for harvesting timber. Always remember that logging-trucks have (*and take*) the right-of-way.

The birding locations in this guide focus on areas that are open to the public. However, many of them are adjacent to closed private property. Please do not travel on any property that is posted as "no trespassing," nor traverse any private property without the landowner's permission. *Stay on the road if there is any doubt in your mind.*

This is a good opportunity to remind birders of the "American Birding Association Code of Ethics". At the front of the book, opposite the Table of Contents, is the complete text of the Code of Ethics. I have summarized it here:

1. Always act in ways that do not endanger the welfare of birds or other wildlife.
2. Always act in ways that do not harm the natural environment.
3. Always respect the rights of others.
4. Birders in groups should assume special responsibilities.

Please be mindful of this code as you bird in New Hampshire. People in rural areas of New Hampshire are generally friendly and are nice folks to meet. However, you will wear out your welcome if you trespass or if you harass wildlife.

Birding Locations by Season

The following table indicates the best seasons during which to visit the various birding locations in the state. For example, if you are visiting New Hampshire during the nesting season, June and July, you can consult the table to quickly locate birding spots which are most active during this season. Each location is also shown on the map at the beginning of this Introduction, with a letter that corresponds to the table.

Birding Area	Map Loc	Spring Mar-May	Nesting Jun-Jul	Fall Aug-Nov	Winter Dec-Feb
Seacoast Loop	A	✔	✔	✔	✔
Isles of Shoals & Pelagics	B	✔	✔	✔	✔
Great Bay Loop	C	✔		✔	✔
Durham - UNH Loop	D	✔	✔	✔	
Pawtuckaway Area	E	✔	✔	✔	
Powwow Pond - Powder House Pond	F	✔	✔	✔	
Lake Massabesic Loop	G	✔	✔	✔	
Hopkinton Lake Loop	H	✔	✔	✔	
Everett Lake Loop	I	✔	✔	✔	
Concord Area	J	✔	✔	✔	
Mount Kearsarge Area	K	✔	✔	✔	
Peterborough Loop	L	✔	✔	✔	
Keene Loop	M	✔	✔	✔	
Lake Winnipesaukee Area	N	✔		✔	
West-Central Lakes	O	✔	✔	✔	
Franconia Notch Loop	P	✔	✔	✔	
Crawford and Jefferson Notches	Q	✔	✔	✔	
Mount Washington	R	✔	✔	✔	
Kancamagus Highway	S	✔	✔	✔	
Connecticut Lakes	T	✔	✔	✔	✔
Lake Umbagog/Androscoggin River	U	✔	✔	✔	✔

A SHORT SCHEDULE

If you have limited time, the following "short schedules" should enable you to visit the best birding locations in the state with the greatest diversity of habitat and species. From spring through fall a short schedule should include: The Seacoast Loop (one day), Pawtuckaway Area (one day), Everett Lake Loop (a half-day), Franconia Notch Loop (one day), Crawford and Jefferson Notches (one day), and the Connecticut Lakes (two days). During winter, try to cover the Seacoast Loop (one day), Great Bay (a half-day), the Connecticut Lakes (one day), and Lake Umbagog and the Androscoggin River (one day).

CAMPING AND LODGING

New Hampshire has numerous campgrounds, both private and state-run. Tourism in the state is very popular during the summer; consequently, campgrounds can be packed, especially on weekends. It is best to write or call ahead to make reservations.

For information on private campgrounds in New Hampshire contact:

- NH Campground Owners' Association
  P.O. Box 320
  Twin Mountain, NH 03595
  603/846-5511

For information on State campgrounds contact:

- NH Division of Parks and Recreation
  P.O. Box 856
  Concord, NH 03302-0856
  603/271-3254

For those who prefer motel accommodations to camping, New Hampshire is still for you. Its popularity as a tourist location assures plenty of lodging throughout the state. There are numerous motels, hotels, cottages, guest houses, and cabins, as well as bed-and-breakfasts.

For information on lodging, dining, and general tourist information on New Hampshire contact:

- NH Office of Vacation Travel
  P.O. Box 856
  Concord, NH 03302-0856
  603/271-2666

Finally, the Appalachian Mountain Club (AMC) operates a number of huts and lodges in New Hampshire, while maintaining hundreds of miles of trails in the state. The AMC is more than that, however. Founded in 1876, the club is the oldest non-profit conservation and outdoor recreation organization in the U.S. The AMC offers workshops at the Pinkham Notch Visitor Center on photography, birding, canoeing, hiking, snowshoeing, cross-country skiing, and many other activities. For information on the AMC contact:

- Appalachian Mountain Club
  5 Joy Street
  Boston, MA 02108
  617/523-0636

or

- Appalachian Mountain Club
  Box 298
  Gorham, NH 03581
  603/466-2727

HOW TO GET HERE

By Air:
Logan International Airport in Boston, Massachusetts, provides a convenient air link from New England to anywhere in the world. All major carriers service Logan International. From Logan, take Interstate 93 or Interstate 95 north for about one hour to southern New Hampshire.

Manchester Municipal Airport is served by a few major carriers (United, Delta, and U.S. Air). Flights in and out of Manchester provide direct access to Boston, New York, Washington, D.C., Chicago, and a few other cities.

By Car:
From the Boston area, a one-hour drive up Interstate 93 or Interststate 95 will find you in southern New Hampshire. Another hour on Interstate 93 and you will be in the White Mountains, prime habitat for northern specialties such as Spruce Grouse, Three-toed and Black-backed Woodpeckers, Gray Jay, Boreal Chickadee, Bicknell's and Swainson's Thrushes, Philadelphia Vireo, and Rusty Blackbird.

SOUTHEASTERN NEW HAMPSHIRE

⭐**A** Seacoast Loop
⭐**B** Isles of Shoals and Pelagic Trips
⭐**C** Great Bay Loop
⭐**D** Durham – University of New Hampshire Loop
⭐**E** Pawtuckaway Area
⭐**F** Powwow Pond – Powder House Pond
⭐**G** Lake Massabesic Loop

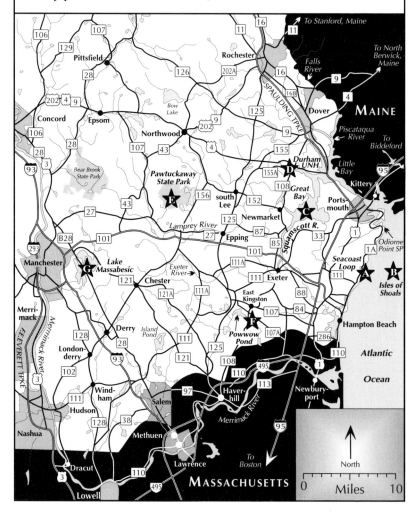

Chapter 1:

SOUTHEASTERN
NEW HAMPSHIRE

This region is defined by a line running from the Tilton/Franklin area south along Interstate 93 to the Massachusetts boundary, and east to Maine and the seacoast. This is the most densely populated area of the state. However, it includes New Hampshire's 18 miles of seacoast and many prime birding areas. Armed with an understanding of the tides, the birder will find that this region can be a particularly wonderful place to bird.

Common and King Eiders
Shawneen E. Finnegan

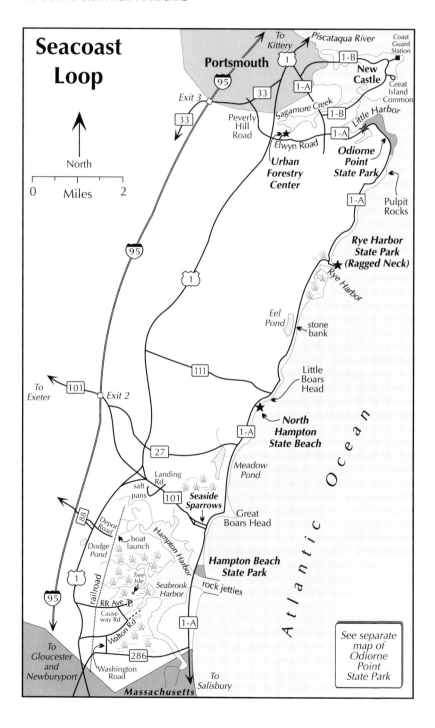

A. SEACOAST LOOP

New Hampshire's 18 miles of seacoast provide rewarding birding in any season. Spring and fall migration are usually productive along the coast, and many nesting species are present during the summer. Waterfowl, hawks, and owls make the seacoast particularly attractive in winter. All traveler services are available in Portsmouth throughout the year and in Hampton primarily during the summer. *Allow a full day for this loop.*

The seacoast tends to be super-crowded on weekends during the summer, especially the area around Hampton Beach. Between Memorial Day and Labor Day it is best to bird the seacoast on a weekday or early in the morning to avoid traffic congestion.

For tourist information on the seacoast region, contact:

- Seacoast Council on Tourism
  1000 Market Street
  Portsmouth, NH 03801
  603/436-7678
  800/221-5623 (outside New Hampshire)

Urban Forestry Center

From Interstate 95 take Exit 3 toward the New Hampshire seacoast, U.S. Highway 1, and State Route 1A. From the end of the exit ramp take State Route 33 east. Go 1.0 mile and turn right at a set of lights onto Peverly Hill Road, which takes you 1.0 mile to U.S. Highway 1 near Yoken's Restaurant. Cross straight over busy U.S. Highway 1 at the lights, onto Elwyn Road. Follow Elwyn Road (east) for 0.2 mile and turn left (north) into the Urban Forestry Center.

This facility is run by the New Hampshire Division of Forests and Lands and is open to the public. The office is open weekdays 8 am to 4 pm; the trails are open daily 7 am to 8 pm. The forestry center encompasses 150 acres of land along the tidal Sagamore Creek. There are picnic tables, trails (with trail guides in the mailbox at the trailhead), and a year-round bird-feeding station that attracts such common species as Downy Woodpecker, Black-capped Chickadee, White-breasted Nuthatch, and House Finch. Concerning this last species, perhaps a few words are in order. After its inadvertent introduction in New York in 1940, the House Finch took another 27 years to reach New Hampshire. Since then, it has spread quickly through cities, suburbs, farmlands, and parks in the southern half of the state and is still spreading northward rapidly.

The trails lead to the marsh at the edge of Sagamore Creek, where in summer you may see Great Blue Heron, Black-crowned Night-Heron, Snowy Egret, and, from November through March, Bufflehead and Common Goldeneye. During spring and fall migration watch the brushy areas for warblers. In winter check the Red Pines for roosting Northern Saw-whet and perhaps Long-eared Owls.

New Castle

As you exit the Forestry Center, turn left (east) to continue on Elwyn Road for 1.2 miles to the junction with State Route 1A. Turn left to go north on 1A for 0.4 mile and then turn right on Route 1B just after the gas station. In 0.8 mile along 1B there is a pull-off on the right that will allow you to view a portion of Little Harbor. Check here for shorebirds and gulls.

Continue on Route 1B for 1.0 mile to Great Island Common (also called New Castle Common). Watch your speed in this area, because the posted limit drops to 25 mph at the New Castle town line, and the local police are in the habit of strictly enforcing it.

This park has a playground, cooking grills, picnic tables, trails, and restrooms (open in summer). There is a small entrance fee in summer. The park affords a good view of Little Harbor where the Piscataqua (pis-CAT-uh-kwah) River flows into the Atlantic Ocean. King Eiders will often winter near the mouth of the river. Winter is also the time to look for Common Loon, Horned and Red-necked Grebes, Great Cormorant, Common Eider, Oldsquaw, all three species of scoter

Coast Guard Station

As you leave Great Island Common, turn right to continue north on State Route 1B. Proceed for 0.4 mile and go straight where Route 1B curves left, following the sign for "Fort Constitution Historic Site" and "U.S.C.G. Station." The Coast Guard station is located at the Revolutionary War-era historic site. In less than 0.1 mile turn right at the entrance to the Coast Guard station. Drive down the entrance road for 100 yards to the parking area on the right.

Walk across the entrance road (to the left), through a section of restricted parking, and out onto the pier where the Coast Guard cutter docks. From the pier you can scan the Piscataqua River for gulls and terns. Look for Laughing and Bonaparte's Gulls, plus Common Terns. Black Terns have been recorded here, and even a rare Little Gull was present in May 1994. During winter look for "white-winged" gulls—Glaucous and Iceland. From spring through fall you may also see Black-crowned Night-Herons. Check the boat-house to the right of the pier for nesting Cliff Swallows in summer.

If you are the kind of birder who enjoys keeping state lists, be aware that all of the birds that are a quarter-mile or more east or north of the Coast Guard station are actually in Maine.

Odiorne Point State Park

Odiorne Point State Park, the largest undeveloped stretch of shore on the state's coast, is productive in spring and fall for land migrants. If you work the brush carefully, you can come up with some great birds. In winter the park is good for offshore waterfowl and seabirds.

Settled by colonists in the 1600s, the land was occupied by the Odiorne family until 1940. The United States Government used this area as a World War II coastal-defense station known as Fort Dearborn, and in 1961 sold it to the State of New Hampshire. As you walk through the park, you will see vestiges of its former use. Note that the gate is open from 8 am until dark (fee).

The Seacoast Science Center, located at Odiorne Point State Park, opened in the summer of 1992. This is a cooperative effort among the Audubon Society of New Hampshire, the New Hampshire Division of Parks, the University of New Hampshire, and the Friends of Odiorne Point. The center is open year round and offers exhibits, aquariums, a nature store, modern restrooms, and nature walks. For more information contact:

- The Seacoast Science Center
  P.O. Box 674, Route 1A
  Rye, NH 03870
  603/436-8043

To reach Odiorne Point from New Castle, return to the junction of State Route 1A and Elwyn Road by bearing left from Route 1B onto 1A south; turn left again as Route 1A turns east. Go east 1.0 mile to a noisy wooden bridge. (The loose planks rattle.) The mudflats by the bridge can be productive for shorebirds at low tide during August and September. Look for Black-bellied and Semipalmated Plovers, Greater and Lesser Yellowlegs, Ruddy Turnstone, Semipalmated and Least Sandpipers, and Short-billed Dowitcher. Besides shorebirds, also check for Double-crested Cormorant; Snowy Egret; Black-crowned Night-Heron;

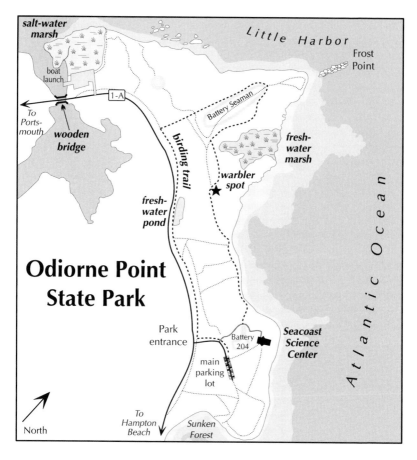

salt-water marsh

Little Harbor

boat launch

Frost Point

1-A

To Portsmouth

wooden bridge

Battery Seaman

fresh-water marsh

birding trail

warbler spot

fresh-water pond

Odiorne Point State Park

Park entrance

Battery 204

Seacoast Science Center

main parking lot

North

To Hampton Beach

Sunken Forest

Atlantic Ocean

American Black Duck; Bonaparte's, Ring-billed, Herring, and Great Black-backed Gulls; Common Tern; Belted Kingfisher; and Tree, Cliff, and Barn Swallows.

In 0.7 mile after the bridge you will come to the main entrance (and fee booth) to Odiorne Point State Park on your left (east). There is a paved parking lot, restrooms, and the Seacoast Science Center. The park is criss-crossed by many walking-paths.

During spring migration a good way to start your exploration is to walk back out the entrance road to Route 1A and walk north along the paved bicycle path which parallels Route 1A. You will pass a freshwater pond, going a total of 0.4 mile, to an old road with a gate across it leading in from Route 1A. Turn right at the gate to walk east on the gravel road. Follow this road past two large World War II-era bunkers, bearing right around the second bunker. Look for the freshwater marsh off to your left (south) that has Virginia Rails. During spring and fall migration you may find Lincoln's Sparrow in the marsh if you are lucky. This species can be secretive. Listen for its bubbly song, similar to that of a House Wren.

Continue along the path as it veers back toward the parking lot. Just past the large maple trees is a dependable place to find warblers during spring migration. Odiorne is probably the very best location in New Hampshire for warbler migration. Look for Northern Parula, Tennessee, Nashville, Magnolia, Cape May, Black-throated Green, Blackburnian, Bay-breasted, Blackpoll, Black-and-white, Mourning, Wilson's, and Canada Warblers, American Redstart, Ovenbird, and Northern Waterthrush.

If you check the undergrowth carefully, you might find (if you are fortunate) a Worm-eating Warbler. Although it is rare in New Hampshire, Kentucky Warbler has also been seen here during spring migration.

Other landbirds to look for at Odiorne include Red-shouldered Hawk, Whip-poor-will, Ruby-throated Hummingbird, Downy and Hairy Woodpeckers, Eastern Wood-Pewee, Yellow-bellied (migrant) and Willow Flycatchers, Eastern Phoebe, House Wren, Ruby-crowned Kinglet (migrant), Swainson's (migrant), Hermit (migrant), and Wood Thrushes, Cedar Waxwing, Solitary Vireo, Northern Cardinal, Rose-breasted Grosbeak, White-throated Sparrow (migrant), Baltimore Oriole, Brown-headed Cowbird, and Purple Finch. In fall you might pick up a White-crowned Sparrow. Odiorne is also a very reliable location for Brown Thrasher.

The tops of the bunkers provide a good locale to watch fall hawk migration. During October this is an especially good spot to view accipiters. You may even see a Peregrine Falcon. May and September are the best times to see Merlins.

During fall migration the best area for passerines is the southern end of the park, south of the main parking lot. There is often a miniature "Cape May effect" as the birds pile up in the trees and undergrowth before continuing across the open ocean and marshes. Although they are rare, you may find Western Kingbird, Orange-crowned and Connecticut Warblers, Yellow-breasted Chat, and Blue Grosbeak. Check any bushes carefully for skulking sparrows. The open grassy areas may produce American Pipits.

There is usually some action on the ocean in any season, but especially in winter. Walk straight out toward the ocean from the parking lot to scope the surf for Red-throated and Common Loons; Horned and Red-necked Grebes; Great Cormorant; Common and King (rare) Eiders; Harlequin Duck (rare); Oldsquaw; Black, Surf, and White-winged Scoters; Common and Barrow's (rare) Goldeneyes; Red-breasted Merganser;

and Bonaparte's Gull. During winter, Odiorne is a likely area in which to find Northern Shrike. For several years recently a Western Grebe has been seen among the Red-necked Grebes wintering off Odiorne Point. Brant is a possibility during spring and fall migration as well.

During late April and early May 1990, a Little Egret was seen along the New Hampshire seacoast. It was first spotted in a small pool along State Route 1A just south of Odiorne Point State Park. It was later found in the Hampton Falls marsh (described in a following section). This was the first New Hampshire record for this species. (It was also one of the first records for North America.)

The entire short New Hampshire seacoast can be productive for wintering waterfowl. As you leave Odiorne Point State Park, continue south on State Route 1A, stopping wherever there is a pull-off with a good view of the ocean. *Pull completely off the road when birding.* During September, any of the beach areas with seaweed (especially Sea Lettuce) may attract migrant shorebirds. A spotting scope is essential.

Glossy Ibises
Shawneen E. Finnegan

Pulpit Rocks

Proceeding south along Route 1A for 0.8 mile you will come to a pull-off on the left at Pulpit Rocks, opposite Pulpit Rock Road. This area is reliable for wintering Red-throated and Common Loons, Horned and Red-necked Grebes, and King Eider. It is also known as the spot where a Western Grebe recently wintered. Harbor Seals will often sun themselves on the off-shore rocks at low tide.

Rye Harbor

Continue south along Route 1A for 2.8 miles to Rye Harbor State Park on Ragged Neck (fee in summer). This small park situated on the northern edge of Rye Harbor has a few picnic tables plus restrooms (open in summer only). It is a worthwhile stop from fall through spring. In late fall and winter look for Horned Lark, Lapland Longspur, and Snow Bunting in the two-acre grassy area beyond the parking lot. During some winters a Snowy Owl can be found here; the bird is usually seen among the rocks on the very stony "beach". Check the large rocks at the entrance to Rye Harbor and at the tip of the neck for Purple Sandpiper. Looking north from Ragged Neck is often a good way to find Barrow's Goldeneye during winter. A Lesser Black-backed Gull was seen in the Harbor in December 1986. September is the time to look in the grassy area for Buff-breasted Sandpiper. During spring and fall watch for Northern Gannet migrating off the coast. Although rare in New Hampshire, a Pacific Loon has been seen offshore from Rye Harbor during fall.

Harlequin Ducks
Barry W. Van Dusen

Upon leaving the park, turn left to continue south on Route 1A for 0.4 mile to the entrance to Rye Harbor State Marina. As you turn left into the marina, you will find no-fee half-hour parking on the left side of the entrance road. Walk out on the dock and scan the harbor for shorebirds, gulls, and terns in season. In winter, check the gulls, particularly for Common Black-headed, Iceland, and Glaucous. There are restrooms next to the dock which are open during the summer.

Rye Harbor and the surrounding area can be a real hotspot for unusual species. Following the passage of a hurricane in fall, interesting southern birds can be seen around the harbor. In August 1991 Hurricane Bob carried a Royal Tern north to Rye Harbor. Be prepared. A friend of mine once found himself in the embarrassing situation of finding a Caspian Tern at Rye Harbor, having plenty of spare film, but no camera!

Just south of the harbor there is an extensive marsh on both sides of the road. This is a reliable location for Great Egret, Little Blue Heron, Black-crowned Night-Heron, and Glossy Ibis. During fall shorebird migration you might find Stilt Sandpiper, Wilson's Phalarope, and other interesting shorebirds. Least and Black Terns pause to fish in the pools during fall migration. An American Avocet has been seen here on at least two occasions.

Eel Pond

Continue south on State Route 1A from Rye Harbor for 1.5 miles to Eel Pond. This is another hotspot for unusual birds. Pull off onto the left side of the road by the Rye Town Beach. (Note that this section has severely restricted parking from Memorial Day through Labor Day.) Climb to the top of the 10-feet-high embankment made of beach stones and gravel to obtain a good view of the freshwater pond. In June and July look for Least Bittern (rare), Green Heron, Glossy Ibis, Wood Duck (nesting), and Marsh Wren. In spring and fall look for migrants such as Pied-billed Grebe, American Bittern, Green-winged Teal, American Black Duck, Blue-winged Teal, Northern Shoveler, Gadwall, Ruddy Duck (rare), American Coot, and Tree, Northern Rough-winged, Bank, Cliff, and Barn Swallows. Fall migration is the time to look for Common Moorhen. Horned Lark and Snow Bunting can often be seen along the edges of Eel Pond during winter. Black-legged Kittiwake is a possibility in winter, especially during or immediately after a winter storm. Clapper Rail has occurred along the New Hampshire coast several times, notably during June and July at Eel Pond.

From the northern end of the stone embankment, where a culvert passes under the road, walk across the road to the edge of Eel Pond. In dry years there may be exposed mudflats at this spot which are reliable for interesting shorebirds, especially during August. Look here for Spotted, Least, White-rumped, Pectoral, and Stilt Sandpipers.

The beach on the ocean-side of the stone embankment is a reliable spot for gulls and shorebirds. In particular, this is a likely place for Sanderling during fall migration. As further evidence of what a hotspot this can be, a Franklin's Gull was seen here recently. Further, a Lesser Black-backed Gull was recorded here in May 1994.

North Hampton State Beach

From Eel Pond follow Route 1A south for 2.2 miles to North Hampton State Beach. Pull into the parking lot on the left. The area of seaweed and Sea Lettuce at the north end of this beach attracts migrant shorebirds, especially during August and September. Migrant shorebirds to look for include Black-bellied Plover, Ruddy Turnstone, Red Knot, Sanderling, Semipalmated, Western, Least, White-rumped, Baird's, and Buff-breasted Sandpipers, and Dunlin. In winter watch for Red-throated and Common Loons, scoters, and Iceland and Glaucous Gulls.

Meadow Pond

Resume your course south on State Route 1A for 1.3 miles to State Route 27. Turn right on Route 27 and go west 0.2 mile to a small red-brick utility building on the left. Pull off here and walk out the path to the right of the building to see Meadow Pond. Look for migrating waterfowl during spring and fall, such as Northern Pintail, Blue-winged Teal, and American Wigeon. During summer look for Green Heron and listen for the rattling song of the Marsh Wren. A Yellow-crowned Night-Heron has been seen here in May and June. This is also a possible location for Least Bittern. You should be able to find a Sora around the pond during fall migration. Return to Route 1A and continue south.

From State Route 27, follow State Route 1A south for 2.0 miles and turn right (west) on the narrow street that is marked as the access to State Route 101. In 0.2 mile turn right into a gravel parking area (between the church and the water-tower). Drive to the edge of the marsh and look for Great Egret, Green Heron, Black-crowned Night-Heron, and Common Tern. This is the only reasonable spot in New Hampshire to look for nesting Seaside Sparrows, and this small colony represents one of the northernmost breeding sites for the species. The Seaside Sparrows here return in mid-May and depart by early October.

In this same area (Hampton Marsh) you can also find nesting Salt-marsh Sharp-tailed Sparrows. These Salt-marsh Sharp-tailed Sparrows are not restricted to the Hampton area, however. They can be found in almost every marsh along the seacoast and even around Great Bay.

The recent splitting of Sharp-tailed Sparrow into two recognized species, Salt-marsh Sharp-tailed Sparrow and Nelson's Sharp-tailed Sparrow, has raised some challenges to birders in New Hampshire. Salt-marsh Sharp-tailed Sparrow is our presumed nester and summer resident. The slightly smaller Nelson's, with its proportionally shorter bill, faintly streaked breast and flanks, and its grayish back with obscure streaking, is a spring and fall migrant through this area; its coastal populations nest farther north. Perfecting the field identification of both "new" species and understanding the arrival and departure dates of both remain to be unraveled by birders here.

Hampton Harbor

As you leave the gravel parking area off the Route 101 access road, turn right, then take a quick left, and go left again to return in 0.2 mile to State Route 1A. Follow Route 1A south for 1.0 mile to Hampton Harbor, which is located just south of Hampton Beach. Look for the brown sign on the right indicating Hampton Harbor State Marina. Hampton Harbor is a reliable place to find migrating and wintering waterfowl such as Common Loon, Great Cormorant, Common Goldeneye, Bufflehead, and Common and Red-breasted Mergansers, but your birding success will vary greatly with the tides—high tide for ducks, low tide for gulls. "Hampton Harbor" is the name given to the Hampton River estuary north of the major bridge over the inlet. It is continuous with Seabrook Harbor (see below), the southern portion of the same estuary.

Hampton Beach State Park

Hampton Beach State Park is practically across the highway (Route 1A) from Hampton Harbor. As you leave the marina, turn right and then make a quick left into the state park. There is a nice beach, a large bath-house, restrooms (open in summer), and a large (approximately 4 acres) grassy area used as a parking area. During summer there is a fee to enter the park, and it is usually far too crowded then for productive birding, anyway. It is during fall and winter that the park provides worthwhile birding. Fall migration is the time to check the beach for Baird's Sandpiper and the grassy areas for Buff-breasted Sandpiper. From spring through fall, the "Ipswich" race of Savannah Sparrow is a possibility on the grassy dunes.

In winter scan the flat grassy area for Horned Lark, Lapland Longspur, and Snow Bunting. Occasionally, a Snowy Owl will sit on one of the buildings or on a nearby dune. From the southeast corner of the park you can scope the inlet to Hampton and Seabrook Harbors. Common Black-headed Gull is a likely prospect in winter. Check the rock jetty for Purple Sandpipers.

Seabrook Harbor

Seabrook Harbor is another reliable place to find shorebirds, gulls, and terns, providing good year-round birding. To reach it from Hampton Beach State Park, continue south on State Route 1A for 0.7 mile, crossing over the harbor inlet bridge. (You can also reach Seabrook Harbor by taking Interstate 95 to State Route 286 to State Route 1A and thus approach the harbor from the south.)

Pull into the paved long parking lot on the west side of Route 1A, 0.4 mile south of the bridge over the inlet to the harbor. On the south side of the harbor the town pier provides a nice vantage point from which to scope the harbor. There should be Double-crested Cormorants around.

Seabrook Harbor at low tide.

Look for gulls: Iceland (winter), Glaucous (winter), Laughing (migration), Bonaparte's, and Ring-billed, among the abundant Herring and Great Black-backed Gulls. An adult Lesser Black-backed Gull was found here in early 1995, also. Don't miss the terns: Roseate (July and August), Common, Arctic (rare migrant), Forster's (July and August), and Least (fall).

Seabrook Harbor is another location with a long record of rarities. Common Black-headed Gull is a winter possibility. In August of 1991, Hurricane Bob deposited a Sandwich Tern in Seabrook Harbor. There are a few Black Skimmer records from the harbor, together with a sighting of two American Oystercatchers from the spring of 1992. A Sabine's Gull was seen here in May 1980, and Little Gulls have visited the harbor in fall. The first confirmed state record of Wilson's Plover was made here in May 1993.

From July through September, this is a rewarding place for shorebird migrants such as American Golden-Plover (rare), Black-bellied and Semipalmated Plovers, Killdeer, Whimbrel, Hudsonian and Marbled (rare) Godwits, Ruddy Turnstone, Red Knot, Sanderling, Semipalmated, Western, Least, White-rumped, and Pectoral Sandpipers, Dunlin, and Short-billed and Long-billed (rare) Dowitchers. If you are lucky, you may even find a Piping Plover. (The most recent confirmed nesting of Piping Plovers at Seabrook goes back to the early 1970s, though they have been observed since, with a probable nesting in 1985. In New Hampshire, as elsewhere, this plover must often struggle for space in the face of people, dogs, and other predators on far too many beaches.)

One way to observe shorebirds in the harbor is to arrive about three hours after high tide, and watch the shorebirds fly in as the tide recedes. The best position for this show is the town pier on the south side of the harbor. Another alternative is to walk out onto the mudflats at low tide, being mindful of the time. Otherwise, the rising tide will catch you. (For reference purposes, high tide along the New Hampshire coast is usually within 10 minutes after Boston high tide.) The best place to cross out onto the mudflats is from just west of the town pier on the south side of the harbor. You should exit the mudflats no later than two hours after the low tide. If you walk out onto the mudflats, be very careful inasmuch as the footing can be unstable. Avoid walking on the mussel-beds or on any areas of the deep black mud where you could get your foot stuck. It is best to stay on the areas of firm gray sand.

A friend once walked out onto the mudflats at low tide and found a Parasitic Jaeger! He become so enthralled with his find that he did not notice the rising tide. When he finally realized that it was well past time to leave, he had to wade waist-deep across the channel that separates the mudflats from the beach.

Seabrook Marsh

From Seabrook Harbor, go south on State Route 1A for 1.1 miles to the traffic light and turn right onto State Route 286. In 0.2 mile pull off to the right near Brown's Seafood Restaurant. Drive out to the gravel area at the edge of the marsh behind the restaurant. This area provides you with a view of the marsh. In winter look for Rough-legged Hawk and Snowy and Short-eared (uncommon) Owls. During spring and fall you may see Great Blue Heron and Great and Snowy Egrets.

As you continue west on Route 286, do not attempt to stop. This section is specifically posted as "emergency stopping only." Go another 1.6 miles west on 286 and turn right at the lights onto Washington Road. In 0.4 mile turn right at the T onto Walton Road. After 0.6 mile the road veers left, but stay straight on Walton Road as it becomes dirt. Go 0.3 mile farther and stop where you have a view of the marsh on both sides of the road. There are several shallow pools on the right (south side) that attract shorebirds during spring and fall migration. Look for Black-bellied and Semipalmated Plovers, Killdeer, Greater and Lesser Yellowlegs, Willet, and Semipalmated, Western, Least, White-rumped, and Pectoral Sandpipers. This is also a reliable area for Green Heron.

Walton Road comes to a dead end just ahead. Turn around and head back to the paved road. Turn right onto Causeway Road and proceed for 0.3 mile to Railroad Avenue. Turn right and go 0.2 mile to a gravel parking lot. There is a paved boat-launch where you can launch a small boat or canoe at high tide. This will allow you access to numerous channels through the marsh. Plan to launch about two hours before high tide. This will allow you about four hours of boating before the tide recedes significantly.

If you arrive at low tide, you can hike the trail that goes off from the northeast corner of the parking lot. The trail leads to the "island" of trees in the marsh. If you decide to walk out into the marsh, watch your step because many ditches remain from the days when an attempt was made to drain the marsh in an effort to control mosquitoes.

During spring and fall migration, if bad weather forces a fallout, this "island" or isolated grove of trees can be full of passerines, including Rufous-sided Towhee and American Tree, Fox, White-throated, and White-crowned Sparrows. In summer, check the marsh for Great and Snowy Egrets, Little Blue, Tricolored (rare), and Green Herons, Black-crowned Night-Heron, Glossy Ibis, and Savannah and Salt-marsh Sharp-tailed Sparrows. During winter the marsh and neighboring woods are likely places to find Sharp-shinned, Cooper's, Red-tailed, and Rough-legged Hawks, American Kestrel, and Great Horned, Snowy, Long-eared (rare), Short-eared, and Northern Saw-whet Owls. If you are *very* lucky you might find a Gyrfalcon in the marsh during February, March, or April.

Heading back up Railroad Avenue for 1.3 miles you will come to U.S. Highway 1. Turn right to go north.

Hampton Falls Marsh

After driving 1.5 miles on U.S. Highway 1, turn left (west) into a gravel area at the edge of Dodge Pond. This spot is worth a quick check for waterfowl during migration. As you leave Dodge Pond, turn left onto U.S. Highway 1 to resume your course northward. In 0.4 mile turn right on Depot Road at the second set of lights (opposite State Route 88). Go 0.7 mile to the end of Depot Road, where you will see a power-line and abandoned railroad tracks through the marsh. This is an excellent birding area, and one of the best places in the state to find herons, egrets, and shorebirds. On August 2, 1992, the second state record for Little Egret was established when one was seen in this marsh by several reliable observers.

Park off to the edge and walk north along the railroad tracks to several small pools (salt pans) on your left. During spring and fall shorebird migration, these pools usually contain a great variety of shorebirds, especially at high tide. The railroad tracks also provide a helpful vantage point of the entire marsh by giving you just enough elevation above the surrounding marsh to help you in scanning for herons and egrets.

Shorebird migrants include American Golden-Plover (rare), Black-bellied and Semipalmated Plovers, Killdeer, Greater and Lesser Yellow-legs, Willet, Whimbrel, Ruddy Turnstone, Spotted, Semipalmated, Western, Least, White-rumped, Pectoral, and Stilt Sandpipers, Short-billed and Long-billed (fall only) Dowitchers, and Wilson's Phalarope (rare). Also during migration watch for Merlin and Peregrine Falcon. In spring, summer, and fall you can find Great and Snowy Egrets, Little Blue and Green Herons, Black-crowned Night-Heron, Glossy Ibis, and Savannah and Salt-marsh Sharp-tailed Sparrows. During winter look for Sharp-shinned and Rough-legged Hawks, and Snowy, Long-eared (rare), Short-eared, and Northern Saw-whet Owls. Year-round residents include Red-tailed Hawk, American Kestrel, Great Horned Owl, and Belted Kingfisher.

From the end of Depot Road, if you drive out over the railroad tracks there is a boat-launch, where you can launch a canoe or row-boat. This mode provides more access to this prime birding habitat through the numerous channels which criss-cross the marsh. Plan to launch about two hours before high tide to give yourself about four hours before the water level in the channels begins to recede again as the tide goes out. (Remember, the high tide here is usually within 10 minutes after Boston high tide.) Navigating the channels through the marsh is an excellent way to find herons and egrets.

Landing Road

Return to U.S. Highway 1, turn right to continue north for 1.0 mile to the junction with State Route 101, and bear right (eastbound) on 101. In 0.5 mile you will come to a 4-way intersection with a set of lights. Turn right onto Landing Road (dead end). Follow Landing Road for 0.5 mile as it curls around to the dead end, where the salt pans are located. At high tide, when the shorebirds are pushed out of Seabrook Harbor, this is a likely spot to re-find them. There are usually numerous Short-billed Dowitchers during August and September. Check the dowitchers carefully, since this is one of the most reliable spots in New Hampshire to find Long-billed Dowitchers. During August or September you might also find a Stilt Sandpiper. Snowy Egret, Green Heron, Glossy Ibis, and Belted Kingfisher also frequent these pools.

This concludes the seacoast loop. From here you can take State Route 101 west to U.S. Highway 1 and Interstate 95, or you can go east to State Route 1A.

If you have time while in the seacoast area, there are many historical sites in Portsmouth that are worth visiting. Strawbery Banke, a 10-acre site along the Piscataqua River, preserves the location of a settlement from 1630. Many old buildings from the 17th and 18th centuries are open to the public. For more information call 603/433-1100. Also be sure to visit one of the many fine seafood restaurants in Portsmouth and Rye for some famous New Hampshire seafood.

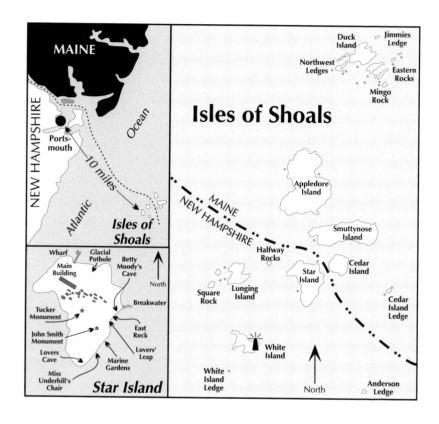

B. ISLES OF SHOALS AND PELAGIC TRIPS

The Isles of Shoals, a group of islands six miles off the New Hampshire coast, provide rewarding year-round birding. Although this archipelago comprises many islands, fewer than half of them are within New Hampshire's borders: Star, Lunging, and White Islands, plus Square Rock. The other islands are actually in the state of Maine.

Star Island, the largest of the New Hampshire islands, is 48 acres in size. It is owned by the Star Island Corporation (since 1916), a joint venture of the Unitarian Universalists and the United Church of Christ. Religious conferences are held on the island at the Star Island Conference Center in the summer and on September weekends.

You can make your own reservations with the Isles of Shoals Steamship Company to reach Star Island. Ask for the "Star Island Stop-over" trip. From mid-June through Labor Day, the *M/V Thomas Laighton* pulls out of Portsmouth Harbor twice a day (currently at 11 am and 2 pm) for Star Island. The 90-foot craft also runs on weekends through September. A limited number of passengers on the morning trip are allowed to disembark on Star Island and remain there, reboarding the ferry on the afternoon trip. With no facilities on the island (other than restrooms), and no provisions for birding visitors to stay overnight on Star, the birding opportunities are restricted by these schedules. Late August and September are the most productive times to bird Star Island for migrants. For information on boat trips contact:

- Isles of Shoals Steamship Company
  315 Market Street, P.O. Box 311
  Portsmouth, NH 03802-0311
  603/431-5500
  800/441-4620 (toll-free from outside NH)
  800/894-5509 (toll-free from inside NH)

There is a small cluster of spruce trees that usually holds fall migrants during September. The rest of the island's vegetation is low scrub trees and bushes, and migrants can be found in any of them. The sparse vegetation is fragile, so it is best to stay on the paths. Besides, Poison Ivy is abundant on the island, making staying on the paths that much easier!

Star Island is a good place to look for unusual migrants such as Clapper Rail (accidental), Red-necked Phalarope, Western Kingbird (fall), Orange-crowned, Cape May, Connecticut (fall), Mourning, Hooded, and Wilson's Warblers, Yellow-breasted Chat (fall), Dickcissel (fall), Clay-colored Sparrow, and Orchard Oriole (May). The second state record for Burrowing Owl was from Star Island. Reminiscent of the Christmas song with the line "a partridge in a pear tree", a Least Bittern was once seen in a pear tree on Star Island.

Approaching Star Island.

Appledore Island, just over the boundary in Maine, hosts a heron-and-egret rookery with several interesting species, including Snowy Egret, Little Blue Heron, Black-crowned Night-Heron, and Glossy Ibis. These birds are often seen foraging along the New Hampshire coast. Additional species nesting on Appledore (and seen in New Hampshire) are Double-crested Cormorant, Common Eider, Herring and Great Black-backed Gulls, and Black Guillemot.

Actually, these latter species nest even on New Hampshire's Isles of Shoals, though not necessarily in large numbers. About 80 pairs of Double-crested Cormorants nest on Square Rock. The two gull species are common nesters on New Hampshire's islands. After an absence of almost a century, Common Eiders resumed nesting on Lunging Island in 1980. Finally, in 1985, New Hampshire's first breeding Black Guillemots were found at a nest site on Star Island. This constitutes the southernmost nesting site for Black Guillemot in North America, or elsewhere for that matter. One former breeding species that has not been found nesting for many years on the Isles of Shoals is the Roseate Tern. Its numbers reached about 50-60 pairs in the late 1930s, but the species was gone by the mid-1950s.

Seabirds found near the islands include Cory's (rare) and Manx Shearwaters, Wilson's Storm-Petrel, Black-legged Kittiwake, Dovekie (rare), Common (rare) and Thick-billed Murres, Razorbill, and Black Guillemot. If you arrive at the coast immediately after a "Nor'easter" (a storm with strong northeast winds), you may find some of these seabirds blown near to the coast.

Wild Beach Roses and warbler spruce trees on Star Island.

Cape May Warbler
Barry W. Van Dusen

Taking a boat trip to Jeffry's Ledge, 20 miles off the coast, is the best way to see pelagic species such as Northern Fulmar, Greater and Sooty Shearwaters, Leach's Storm-Petrel (rare), Red Phalarope, Pomarine, Parasitic, and Long-tailed (rare) Jaegers, and Great Skua (rare).

For information on boat trips to Jeffry's Ledge, contact the Isles of Shoals Steamship Company (listed above) or:

- NH Seacoast Cruises
  P.O. Box 232
  Rye Harbor, NH 03870
  603/964-5545 or 603/382-6743
  800/872-4753 (toll-free from outside NH)
  800/734-6488 (toll-free from inside NH)

The best dates for productive birding for pelagic species are probably from late July through September.

Note that these boat trips are primarily for whale-watching; birds are not the primary focus. Be sure to call ahead first to find out if the boat is going to Jeffry's Ledge. If the boat is heading for deep water, you are unlikely to see many birds. (Also, if it goes up the coast to Maine, then you cannot count the birds on your New Hampshire list.) Since the abundance of pelagic birds can vary, be sure to ask if they have been seeing any birds lately. Whales that you are likely to see include Humpback, Finback, Northern Right, and Minke. In 1993, a surprising Blue Whale was seen. You should also see Atlantic White-sided Dolphin.

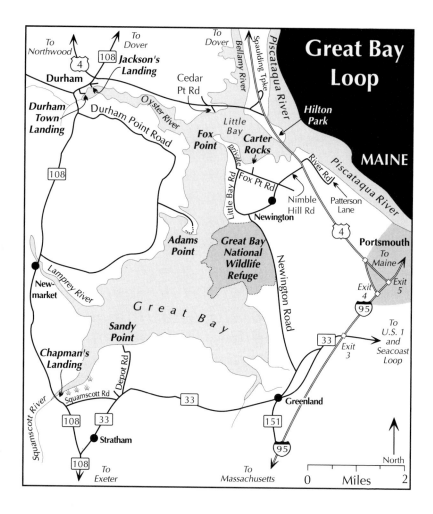

C. GREAT BAY LOOP

Slightly inland from the New Hampshire coastline is a remarkable area known as Great Bay. The largest inland saltwater bay on the East Coast, it is located fully ten miles up the Piscataqua River, so far inland that many visitors imagine that the bay is freshwater. With spring runoff from three rivers, the bay can be almost full of fresh water, and then the salt levels in the bay can change strikingly. But it is the river flow and the twice-daily six-to-eight-foot tides that bring a rich cycle of nutrients into the estuary system. The upshot is a rich life for fishes, oysters, shrimp, and crabs, and a resulting magnet for birdlife.

Great Bay provides fruitful birding during spring, fall, and winter. In spring and fall expect migrating herons, egrets, waterfowl, and passerines. As noted, Great Bay is tidal, exposing mudflats at low tide. High tide in the bay is about two hours after Boston high tide, with low tide about six hours before and after high tide. In fall the waterfowl and shorebird migrations are especially productive. Great Bay has the highest concentration of wintering Bald Eagles in the state. December through March is the time to look for the eagles as well as for wintering waterfowl. A scope is essential when birding Great Bay. *Allow at least a half-day for this trip,* which will take you on a complete loop around the bay. All traveler services are found in Durham, Newington, and Portsmouth.

Jackson's Landing

From the junction of U.S. Highway 4 and State Route 108 in Durham, go south on Route 108 for 0.1 mile and turn left on Old Piscataqua Road, and then take an immediate right at the sign for Jackson's Landing. This short road leads to a large parking area and a paved boat-launch on the Oyster River. This is an easy spot from which to launch a canoe or other boat on the river, which flows to Little Bay. The dock provides a good site from which to scan for birds. Look for Double-crested Cormorant, Great Blue Heron, Ring-billed, Herring, and Great Black-backed Gulls, and American Crow. This is also a reliable spot for the introduced Mute Swan, a species that has been spreading recently. The first recorded breeding for Mute Swan in New Hampshire was in 1968. Into the 1970s the Coastal New Hampshire Christmas Bird Count would regularly record a couple of birds; this increased to a handful in the 1980s, and now that count tallies at least a couple of dozen. As we have seen at other locations on the Atlantic Coast, this aggressive species has become a problem bird, competing too successfully with our native waterfowl.

Durham Town Landing

Return to State Route 108 and turn left, and in 0.3 mile go left onto Landing Road. Follow Landing Road for 0.2 mile and then turn left into the Durham Town Landing on the Oyster River. There is a small park with picnic tables, park benches, and a clear view of the river. The birds are about the same as those listed for Jackson's Landing, but also look for Hooded Merganser and Northern Goshawk. During spring you may also hear Fish Crow around Durham. Be alert for their nasal *aw-aw* call, because this bird is best identified by voice. Fish Crows first nested in New Hampshire on the University of New Hampshire campus in Durham (behind Kendall Hall) in 1982, though they had been present on the campus since 1977. Durham remains the best place to find Fish Crows in the state. They especially favor the tall trees abutting the Durham Shopping Mall.

Adams Point

Return to State Route 108, turn left, and in 0.2 mile bear left at the traffic island to stay on Route 108. In 0.4 mile turn left on Durham Point Road. Follow this road for 3.6 miles and turn left through the metal gate onto Adams Point Road (unmarked). Adams Point in the past supported a family farm, a hotel, a brickyard, and a shipyard. Today it is the home of the University of New Hampshire's Jackson Estuarine Laboratory for marine research. Drive slowly and carefully since the road is narrow. As you drive this stretch, listen for Pileated Woodpecker and a variety of passerines. From mid-May to mid-June watch along the edge of the road for Pink Lady's-slipper (Moccasin-flower). *This orchid species is protected by law, so please do not pick any of them.*

As you proceed out Adams Point Road, in 0.8 mile you will come to a pull-off on the left. Stop here with Little Bay on your left and a tidal

Little Bay as seen from Adams Point.

marsh of Great Bay on your right. There is a boat-launch on the left where you can launch a canoe or other small boat (at high tide). The salt pans on the right are productive during fall migration for herons, egrets, and shorebirds. Look for Great Blue Heron, Great and Snowy Egrets, Green Heron, Glossy Ibis, Semipalmated Plover, Greater and Lesser Yellowlegs, Solitary, Semipalmated, Least, and Baird's Sandpipers, and American Pipit. In spring and summer listen for Brown Thrasher as it performs each of its calls twice from the nearby woods.

During fall and winter scan Little Bay to your left for waterfowl. There are usually flocks of Canada Geese and American Black Ducks here. In November look for Horned Grebe and Ruddy Duck (rare). Throughout the winter look for Mallard, Greater and Lesser Scaups, Common Gold-eneye, Bufflehead, and Common and Red-breasted Mergansers. You should easily pick up Mute Swans here, too.

Continue out Adams Point Road for another 0.3 mile and park in the lot at the Jackson Estuarine Laboratory. Walk down behind the lab building and around to the left toward the boat dock. The dock provides a convenient position from which to scope the bay. One winter, from this spot, I observed an opportunistic Bald Eagle feeding on a Herring Gull. Seeing the eagle from here was no accident, since Adams Point is an excellent spot to watch for eagles in winter. Also in winter, check the gulls in the area carefully for Iceland and Glaucous.

Walk back toward the parking lot and follow the path to the left that leads out through the field to the bay. Check around the field for Northern Harrier (migrant), Broad-winged Hawk, Eastern Phoebe, Eastern King-bird, Tree and Barn Swallows, Blue-gray Gnatcatcher, Eastern Bluebird, Northern Mockingbird, Brown Thrasher, Black-and-white Warbler, Rose-breasted Grosbeak, Song Sparrow, Bobolink, and Eastern Meadowlark. During fall and winter this is a likely spot for Northern Shrike and American Tree Sparrow.

Continue through the field to the edge of the bay. In winter this is another reliable place to observe Bald Eagles. Scope the tops of any dead trees on the opposite shore, which is Woodman Point on the Great Bay National Wildlife Refuge. Bald Eagles will often roost there in the morning. By the late afternoon the eagles may return to roosting sites just south of Adams Point. Also check the trees on the island to the right. Remember to scan the surface of the bay for waterfowl and seabirds. A rarity in New Hampshire, a Tundra Swan was seen on Great Bay during a December Christmas Bird Count in 1985. If you are extremely lucky, you might find a Greater White-fronted Goose mixed in with the flocks of Canada Geese.

Eastern Screech-Owl
Barry W. Van Dusen

The path continues to skirt the field along the edge of the bay and leads to the woods. At low tide it is worthwhile to scramble down the bank and continue walking along the edge of the bay to where the field ends at the woods. This route will provide you with better views of the bay.

During spring and fall migration look for Red-throated Loon, Horned and Red-necked Grebes, Brant (rare), American Wigeon, Canvasback, Ring-necked Duck, Greater Scaup, Common Goldeneye, and Common and Red-breasted Mergansers. Eurasian Wigeons have been seen on Great Bay a few times. Check any flocks of American Wigeons carefully, in case there is a Eurasian mixed in with them.

Chapman's Landing

Return to Durham Point Road, turn left, and proceed for 3.8 miles to Main Street in Newmarket. Turn left on Main Street, which is also State

Route 108. In 0.4 mile bear left at the blinking light to stay on Route 108. Follow State Route 108 for another 2.8 miles (passing through Newfields and into Stratham), and then immediately after crossing the bridge over the Squamscott River turn left into Chapman's Landing. The New Hampshire Fish and Game Department manages a boat-launch here with a large parking lot and latrines.

This spot affords you a view of the extensive marsh alongside the Squamscott River as it flows north toward Great Bay. This is also a convenient place to launch a canoe or other boat to further explore the marsh. The high tide here is about three hours after the coastal (Boston) high tide. Species to look for include Snowy Egret, Little Blue Heron, Glossy Ibis, Northern Harrier (migrant), Spotted and Semipalmated Sandpipers, and Salt-marsh Sharp-tailed Sparrow. During April, May, and August, flocks of Glossy Ibises numbering up to 50 have been seen in this marsh.

Among the Glossy Ibises on April 15, 1995, was the state's very first record of White-faced Ibis. The bird was a "one-day wonder," but fortunately many local birders were called and were able to convene at the site.

Starting in 1993, Ospreys have nested on a utility pole at the far end of the marsh. They are visible from the parking area by looking northeast. A spotting scope is helpful.

Sandy Point

Upon leaving Chapman's Landing, turn left to continue south on State Route 108 for 0.2 mile, where you should turn left onto Squamscott Road. Immediately after turning onto Squamscott Road, one has a good view of the marsh. Follow this road for 1.1 miles until it ends at State Route 33. Turn left onto busy Route 33, go 0.2 mile, and turn left onto Depot Road (this will be your second left off Route 33). In 0.8 mile turn left onto Tidewater Farm Road. Follow this road for 0.2 mile as it curves right, crosses the railroad tracks, and winds its way to the New Hampshire Fish and Game access area.

You will find an Interpretive Center at Sandy Point with exhibits and information on Great Bay. A nature trail including a 1,500-foot boardwalk will help you to view the bay. There is also a public boat-ramp. There is usually a large flock of Greater Scaup out on the bay from fall through spring. During November and March be on the lookout for a Redhead mixed in with the Greater Scaup. Brant are occasionally seen during November, associating with the large flocks of Canada Geese.

Other wintering waterfowl species to look for include Common Gold-eneye, Bufflehead, and Common and Red-breasted Mergansers. A flock of up to 50 Mute Swans has been on Great Bay in the past few years (from fall through spring), and you can easily spot them from Sandy Point. Here in November 1994 my wife and I found the first Eurasian Wigeon (an immature male) seen in New Hampshire in forty years.

You should check the brushy areas around the Interpretive Center for Downy Woodpecker, Northern Flicker, Tufted Titmouse, White-breasted Nuthatch, American Robin, Northern Mockingbird, Cedar Waxwing, Northern Cardinal, and Purple Finch.

Carter Rocks

Return on Depot Road to State Route 33. Turn left onto Route 33 and drive 3.6 miles to a set of lights at the junction with State Route 151. Turn left at the lights and after 0.7 mile bear left onto Newington Road. Proceed for 3.6 miles, passing into Newington, to a T in the road. Turn left onto Little Bay Road and in 1.1 miles you will come to Fox Point Road. Searching the trees near this junction may turn up an Eastern Screech-Owl or a Northern Saw-whet Owl.

Turn right onto Fox Point Road, go 0.2 mile, and turn left on Carter's Lane. In 0.2 mile the road ends at Carter Rocks, where there are a small pine grove and a good view of Little Bay. You may find an Eastern Screech-Owl or a Northern Saw-whet Owl in these pines, also.

Your owl-searching in the Carter Rocks area might be productive at any time of year, but is more likely to be successful in winter.

Hilton Park

Return to Fox Point Road, turn left, and go 0.6 mile to a blinking red light. Turn left at the light onto Nimble Hill Road and go 0.7 mile to U.S. Highway 4. You must turn right to take U.S. Highway 4 heading southeast. Move into the left lane quickly, and in 0.3 mile go left at the "Reverse Direction". After reversing direction to head northwest on U.S. Highway 4, go 0.4 mile and take Exit 4. Make a quick right onto River Road, proceed 0.8 mile, and turn left onto Patterson Lane. In 0.5 mile the road ends at a cul-de-sac along the Piscataqua River. Scan the river for migrant and wintering waterfowl such as Common Loon, Bufflehead, and Red-breasted Merganser.

Return to River Road and go back to where you exited from U.S. Highway 4. Follow U.S. Highway 4 northwest for 0.5 mile, over the bridge into Dover, take Exit 5, and turn into Hilton Park. There is a boat-launch, a playground, picnic tables, and a view of the Piscataqua River. To reach the boat-launch stay to the right and drive straight down to where the river passes under U.S. Highway 4. Check again for waterfowl.

Return to U.S. Highway 4 and drive northwest again; in 0.7 mile take Exit 6w and loop around to stay on U.S. Highway 4 west. In 1.3 miles, after crossing the Bellamy River into Durham, take a sharp left at the 4-way intersection onto Cedar Point Road. This is a small road and easy to miss. Follow Cedar Point Road for 0.2 mile and bear right on the dirt road to the boat-launch. This spot provides another view of Little Bay.

Return to U.S. Highway 4, turn left, and go 2.4 miles back to the loop's starting-point at the junction of U.S. Highway 4 and State Route 108 in Durham.

As a side-trip, there is an unique natural history museum in downtown Dover, the Woodman Institute. A three-building complex located at 182 Central Avenue, it is open every afternoon (2 pm to 5 pm), except on Sundays and Mondays, when it is closed. The Woodman House has an excellent old collection of birds, eggs, nests, and Native American artifacts. It's a museum well worth visiting and is free of charge.

Great Bay National Wildlife Refuge

Over a thousand acres of the former Pease Air Force Base, in Newington, is being turned into a national wildlife refuge. Given that most of the land around the Great Bay is privately held and developed, the decommissioning of the base in 1989 provided a fabulous opportunity to set aside and preserve a large tract of unique and special habitat on the Bay.

The refuge provides critical habitat for migrant waterfowl, nesting Ospreys, wintering Bald Eagles, and many passerines. A flock of Wild Turkeys also inhabits the refuge. The only known nesting location in the state for Upland Sandpiper is the grassland adjacent to the airport runway (not publicly accessible). In the future, refuge personnel hope to encourage Upland Sandpipers to nest on refuge property.

A limited portion of the refuge is open to the public. For up-to-date information contact:

- Great Bay National Wildlife Refuge
  336 Nimble Hill Road
  Newington, NH 03801
  603/431-7511

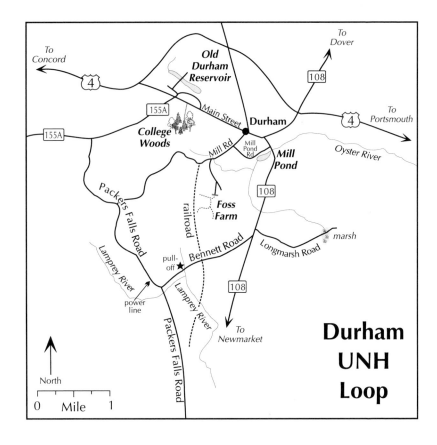

D. DURHAM — UNH LOOP

There are several worthwhile birding locations around the University of New Hampshire's main campus in Durham. Spring, summer, and fall are all productive times to bird this area, which is especially rewarding for finding warblers and other passerines. There are stores, restaurants, and gas stations in downtown Durham. The New England Center, run by the University, provides elegant dining, plus accommodations. Portsmouth is also nearby and can provide all services for the traveler. *Allow a half-day for this loop.*

Foss Farm

From one-way Main Street in downtown Durham turn right onto Mill Road. After 1.0 mile on Mill Road, turn left onto Foss Farm Road, go 0.3 mile, and turn right onto a narrow dirt road. Drive 0.2 mile down to a metal gate. Park along the edge of the road. *Do not block the gate.* The Foss Farm property is owned by the University of New Hampshire and includes old fields as well as wooded areas, but no farm buildings. Foss Farm is one of the best places in southern New Hampshire to find warblers. Knowing your bird songs and calls will give you an advantage here, since many species are much more easily heard than seen.

Just beyond the metal gate the path forks. Bear right and walk about 100 feet; turn left onto a path between two large maple trees. In about a quarter-mile you will come to a fork in the path with a large White Pine tree in the middle of the fork. Bear left and walk another quarter-mile through a few logging clearings.

The edges of these cleared areas attract a variety of birds (mostly nesting), including Sharp-shinned and Red-shouldered Hawks; Ruffed Grouse; Downy and Hairy Woodpeckers; Northern Flicker; Eastern Wood-Pewee; White-breasted Nuthatch; Blue-gray Gnatcatcher; Solitary and Yellow-throated Vireos; Blue-winged, Golden-winged (uncommon), Chestnut-sided, Magnolia (migrant), Cape May (migrant), Black-throated Green, Pine, Prairie, Bay-breasted (migrant), and Black-and-white Warblers; Common Yellowthroat; Rose-breasted Grosbeak; Indigo Bunting; Rufous-sided Towhee; and White-throated Sparrow. You may even find an Orchard Oriole in this area if you are lucky.

Return to the fork by the large White Pine and turn left to take the other side of the fork. As you walk out this path, you will pass old overgrown fields. A Barred Owl is often heard in this area. In about a half-mile you will come to a stream-crossing. Listen for Olive-sided (spring migrant) and Least Flycatchers, Veery, Wood Thrush, Nashville Warbler (migrant), Ovenbird, Louisiana Waterthrush, Mourning Warbler (migrant), and Scarlet Tanager.

Backtrack on this path to the point where you turned left between the two large maple trees. If you turn right here, you will return to the metal gate by the parking area. If you turn left, you will pass an old graveyard on the left and come to a power-line along the edge of the Boston and Maine Railroad. Regular nesters in this area include Gray Catbird, Blue-winged and Prairie Warblers, Rose-breasted Grosbeak, Rufous-sided Towhee, and Field Sparrow. Pileated Woodpeckers and American Woodcock are also found here.

Mill Pond

Return on Mill Road to the center of Durham. Turn right and continue straight out from the center of town. In 0.2 mile bear right to go south on State Route 108 toward Newmarket. In 0.1 mile turn right onto Mill Pond Road and in another 0.1 mile pull off on the right, opposite Mill Pond. This is a reliable nesting spot for Mute Swan. Also look for Little Blue Heron, American Wigeon (during migration), and Chimney Swift. There are benches and picnic tables along the edge of the pond. This area is very near the Durham Town Landing and the Durham Shopping Mall, and thus is part of the most reliable place in the state to find Fish Crow. Listen for its distinctive nasal and staccato *aw-aw* call. Unless the nasal call is very short, you could be fooled by a young American Crow; this caution is especially important during the period of late June to early September.

Longmarsh Road

Return to State Route 108, turn right, and continue for 1.3 miles, turning left onto Longmarsh Road. Go 1.1 miles to a large cattail marsh on the right. (Longmarsh Road changes from paved to dirt half way to the marsh.)

Mill Pond Dam.

This marsh has Least Bittern (rare), Virginia Rail, and Sora. If you arrive in early morning or late afternoon, you may be treated to a Beaver making its rounds through the marsh.

Species found in the surrounding woods include White-breasted Nuthatch, Blue-gray Gnatcatcher (uncommon), Cedar Waxwing, Red-eyed Vireo, Black-throated Green Warbler, Scarlet Tanager, and Baltimore Oriole. During spring and summer evenings listen for Whip-poor-wills. If you are alert, you may hear a Ruffed Grouse "drumming".

Packers Falls

Return to State Route 108 and go diagonally across the street to Bennett Road. As you drive along this road, watch the fields for Eastern Bluebird, Bobolink, and Eastern Meadowlark. Follow Bennett Road for

Eastern Bluebirds
Barry W. Van Dusen

0.8 mile and pull off on the left just before the railroad bridge where a small power-line crosses the road. The power-line intersects with another on the right side of the road. This is a reliable spot for typical power-line species such as Gray Catbird, Blue-winged, Golden-winged (uncommon), Yellow, Chestnut-sided, and Prairie Warblers, Indigo Bunting, Rufous-sided Towhee, and Field Sparrow.

Continue on Bennett Road for another 0.4 mile to a pull-off on the right side, just after the guard rail. There is a stream-crossing here that joins the Lamprey River just below Packers Falls. You can bird this area from both sides of the road. This is a fairly reliable location for nesting Louisiana Waterthrush. Other nesting birds include: Willow and Great Crested Flycatchers, Warbling Vireo, Black-and-white Warbler, and Scarlet Tanager.

Another 0.4 mile on Bennett Road will bring you to Packers Falls Road. Turn right and go 0.2 mile to a small power-line crossing the road. The power-line right-of-way is very overgrown, so you may not want to walk out along it. However, you can hear and see many birds from the road. Listen for Gray Catbird, Blue-winged, Chestnut-sided, and Black-and-white Warblers, American Redstart, Ovenbird, Common Yellow-throat, Rose-breasted Grosbeak, Indigo Bunting, and Rufous-sided Towhee. This is one of the most reliable locations in New Hampshire for Golden-winged Warbler.

Golden-winged Warbler is a rare breeding bird in New Hampshire. As overgrown farms actually dwindle in the state, so do the territories of the Golden-winged Warbler. Tied to successional habitat—often in moist, brushy meadows adjacent to deciduous woods—this species is now most often found along power-line rights-of-way. These warblers arrive in mid-May, and quickly establish territories, marked with their buzzy songs. When present, and singing, this warbler responds well to "pishing." The males, however, cease their singing in mid-June and soon become difficult to find. The warblers will usually depart by early September.

Old Reservoir

Continue on Packers Falls Road for 2.6 miles to the junction with State Route 155A. Turn right and go 1.3 miles. At the stop-sign where State Route 155A makes a sharp left, go straight across and in 0.1 mile turn left onto Spinney Lane; then in another 0.1 mile turn right (toward the UNH Horticulture Farm). After just 0.2 mile you will come to the old Durham

Reservoir. There is a large pull-off area on the right side of the road, where you can see water on both sides.

The combination of woods, water, and nearby fields makes this an excellent place to find birds during spring, summer, and fall. Look for American Kestrel, Downy Woodpecker, Eastern Wood-Pewee, Eastern Phoebe, Eastern Kingbird, American Crow, Black-capped Chickadee, Tufted Titmouse, Red-eyed Vireo, Pine and Wilson's (migrant) Warblers, and Song Sparrow.

College Woods

Return to the junction with State Route 155A and turn left to head back toward downtown Durham. In 0.2 mile pull off on the right by a small woods road immediately after the UNH sign but before the athletic fields. There is a series of paths which criss-crosses this wooded area owned by the University. You can reach the new Durham Reservoir on the Lamprey River by following these paths. Enter College Woods by walking the old woods road which skirts the edge of the athletic fields and passes by a small observatory dome on your left.

Look for Killdeer (on the edge of the athletic fields), Great Horned and Barred Owls, Northern Flicker, Swainson's Thrush (in migration), and wood warblers.

Red-bellied Woodpeckers have been known to winter at feeders in the Durham area. There are between three and seven sightings of this species in the state each year. Another feeder bird to look for around Durham is the Dickcissel—rare but annual in small numbers—which will mix in with flocks of House Sparrows during fall and winter. Recently, Carolina Wrens have moved into the area and may overwinter at feeding stations. As always, remember to respect private property.

This is the end of the Durham-UNH loop. Drive past the athletic fields and the field-house to return to downtown Durham.

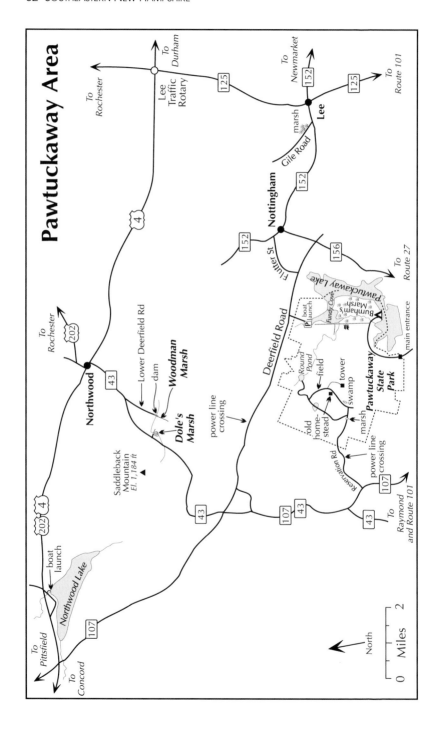

Pawtuckaway Area

E. PAWTUCKAWAY AREA

The main feature of this trip is Pawtuckaway State Park, which encompasses a 5,500-acre natural area, including 800-acre Lake Pawtuckaway. The tent camping area at the park is open from late May through Columbus Day. For information on camping and other park facilities call 603/895-3031. This area provides good birding during spring and fall migration as well as during the summer nesting season. *Allow a full day for this trip.*

Gile Road Marsh

From the junction of State Routes 125 and 152 in Lee, go west on Route 152 for 0.4 mile, turn right onto Gile Road, and stop at the large marsh 0.2 mile on the right. Look for Green Heron, Wood Duck, American Black Duck, Osprey (in migration), Red-shouldered Hawk, Virginia Rail, Chimney Swift, Tree, Bank, Cliff, and Barn Swallows, Common Yellowthroat, Swamp Sparrow, and Red-winged Blackbird. From the woods opposite the marsh you are more likely to hear than to see Eastern Wood-Pewee, Great Crested Flycatcher, Red-breasted and White-breasted Nuthatches, Red-eyed Vireo, Yellow-rumped and Black-and-white Warblers, Ovenbird, Scarlet Tanager, Northern Cardinal, and

Gile Road Marsh.

Rufous-sided Towhee. During summer the marsh comes into bloom with Yellow Pond-lily (or Spatterdock) and both the white and rare pink forms of Fragrant Water-lily.

Fundy Cove

Return to State Route 152 and continue west. In 3.0 miles you will come to the junction with State Route 156, in Nottingham. Continue on Route 152 for another 0.2 mile and turn left onto Flutter Street, which goes 1.1 miles to end at Deerfield Road. Turn right and proceed for 1.0 mile to an unmarked dirt road on the left. This 0.5-mile road leads to a boat-launch at Fundy Cove on Pawtuckaway Lake.

This is a nice spot to launch a canoe or row-boat to explore the lake. This is also a good starting-point to hike a few trails to look (and listen) for woodland birds such as Downy and Hairy Woodpeckers, Tufted Titmouse, Winter Wren, Hermit Thrush, Solitary Vireo, and Black-throated Green, Pine, Black-and-white, and Canada Warblers. Pawtuckaway is a reliable area for nesting Yellow-bellied Sapsuckers. Listen carefully for their *mew* call.

Walk past the metal gate, just to the right of the boat-launch, and over the bridge. Continue straight, following this trail to the south for about a half-mile to a small path on the left leading out to the edge of Fundy Cove. (You can also catch a glimpse of Burnham's Marsh off to the right.)

Chestnut-sided Warbler
Barry W. Van Dusen

Continue on the main trail for another few hundred feet to trail-marker number 11. Turn right here and walk a quarter-mile to a stream-crossing and a marshy area. Look for Great Blue Heron and Belted Kingfisher.

When you return to trail-marker 11, you can turn left to return to the parking lot at the boat-launch, or you can turn right to follow the trail southwest along the edge of Burnham's Marsh. In about a mile this trail leads to the paved road near the group camping and picnicking area.

From the parking area at the boat-launch, return to Deerfield Road and turn left. In 3.0 miles you will come to a power-line crossing. This is a good spot to stop and check for birds such as Black-billed Cuckoo, Eastern Kingbird, Gray Catbird, Nashville, Chestnut-sided, and Prairie Warblers, Common Yellowthroat, Rose-breasted Grosbeak, Rufous-sided Towhee, and Field Sparrow. Watch the sky for soaring Turkey Vultures.

Dole's Marsh

Resume your route along Deerfield Road and in 1.6 miles stay right at the fork and drive another 0.8 mile to the junction of Routes 107 and 43. Turn right on Route 43 and proceed for 2.0 miles to a marsh on the left side of the road. Pull off here and take a quick look at the marsh. As you drive along this section of State Route 43, you can see Saddleback Mountain off to your left.

Continue for another 1.0 mile to the Northwood town line at a stream-crossing under the road. In just 0.1 mile after the town line, turn right onto an unmarked dirt road which leads a short distance to Dole's Marsh in Woodman State Forest. Park near the dam and check the marsh for such regular species as Great Blue Heron, Wood Duck, Belted Kingfisher, Great Crested Flycatcher, Barn Swallow, Common Yellow-throat, and Red-winged Blackbird. There are also Beavers in the marsh.

Woodman Marsh

Return to State Route 43, turn right, go 1.2 miles, and take a sharp right onto Lower Deerfield Road. In 0.9 mile you will come to a small parking area next to a sign for Woodman Marsh – NH Fish and Game Waterfowl Management Area. Check for typical marsh birds, such as those at Dole's Marsh. Beyond the dam the road becomes too rough to drive, but you can walk along it to bird more of Woodman State Forest.

Ring-necked Ducks
Barry W. Van Dusen

Northwood Lake

Return to State Route 43, turn right, and go 1.3 miles to U.S. Highway 4. Turn left to follow U.S. Highway 4 for 5.7 miles and turn left at a small crossroads. Take an immediate left into the gravel boat-launch on the edge of Northwood Lake.

Bird along the edge of the trees for species such as Black-capped Chickadee, Tufted Titmouse, Gray Catbird, and Yellow-throated and Red-eyed Vireos. Scope the lake for nesting Common Loons and American Black Ducks. During spring and fall waterfowl migration, look for species such as Green-winged Teal, Canvasback (uncommon), Ring-necked Duck, Lesser Scaup, all three scoters, Common Goldeneye, Bufflehead, and Hooded and Common Mergansers.

As you leave the boat-launch, turn left and drive slowly through the 0.8-mile loop that takes you back to U.S. Highway 4. You will pass several good vantage points where you can see the lake from the road.

Pawtuckaway State Park

Turn left onto U.S. Highway 4, drive 1.2 miles, and turn left on State Route 107. Follow State Route 107 south for 9.8 miles to Reservation Road. Turn left onto Reservation Road at the small brown Pawtuckaway

State Park sign indicating the way to the lookout tower. After 1.0 mile the road becomes dirt, and in another 0.1 mile you will come to a power-line crossing with easy access on both sides of the road. Stop at the power-line right-of-way to look for Gray Catbird, Chestnut-sided, Pine, Prairie, and Black-and-white Warblers, Common Yellowthroat, Rufous-sided Towhee, and Field Sparrow. Listen for Hairy and Pileated Woodpeckers, Veery, Hermit Thrush, and Solitary Vireo in the adjacent woods. Watch the sky for Turkey Vultures, and listen for the guttural calls of the Common Raven.

Continue along Reservation Road; in 0.1 mile bear right at the fork, and in 1.0 mile stop at a small marsh visible on both sides of the road. About 100 feet past the marsh there is a trail leading into the woods on the right side of the road. This short path is an excellent place to look for flycatchers, nuthatches, vireos, and warblers.

Another 0.2 mile along Reservation Road will bring you to a T in the road. Turn left toward the lookout tower, and proceed 0.3 mile to a large swamp on the right. Park off to the edge of the road and bird along the edge of the swamp and down to the next bend in the road.

This area attracts a great diversity of nesting species, including some that are usually thought of as more "northern," such as Yellow-bellied Sapsucker, Red-breasted Nuthatch, Winter Wren, Black-throated Green Warbler, Northern Waterthrush, Purple Finch, and White-throated Sparrow. Yellow-bellied Flycatcher is usually easy to find in migration if you are familiar with its call. Ruby-crowned Kinglet is a common migrant.

You can also expect nesting Belted Kingfisher, Downy, Hairy, and Pileated Woodpeckers, Eastern Wood-Pewee, Least and Great Crested Flycatchers, Tufted Titmouse, White-breasted Nuthatch, Brown Creeper, Blue-gray Gnatcatcher, Veery, Hermit Thrush, Solitary, Yellow-throated, and Red-eyed Vireos, Chestnut-sided and Black-and-white Warblers, American Redstart, Common Yellowthroat, Scarlet Tanager, Indigo Bunting, and Swamp Sparrow. You may even find Northern Saw-whet Owl.

After thoroughly exploring the area near the swamp, driving another 0.4 mile will bring you to the trailhead (on the right) that leads to the lookout tower. There is usually room to park a few cars here. A Cerulean Warbler has been a regular in this immediate area in recent years. Listen for its song, which is similar to that of the Black-throated Blue Warbler. However, be sure to *see* the bird, because one of the numerous local American Redstarts sings a fine copy of the normal song of the Cerulean. (This is a widespread phenomenon which has produced some dubious records of Ceruleans elsewhere.) This is the most reliable area in New

Hampshire to find the Cerulean now, although there used to be two individuals about a mile to the west.

Along the trail to the tower listen for Swainson's Thrush during spring migration. You should be able to find Dark-eyed Juncos in summer. The base of the tower is at an elevation of 908 feet. This altitude presents you with an impressive panorama of southeastern New Hampshire. Look for Turkey Vultures and Common Ravens. The tower also provides a good viewing-site for observing fall hawk migration during September and October.

Diagonally opposite from the tower parking area you will find the remnants of an old homestead from the 19th century. Still visible are the foundation, a root-cellar, and the old family graveyard. Louisiana Waterthrush can be heard near the stream just below the old cellar-hole 100 feet down the hill. Lilacs, Rhubarb, Day-lilies, and Forsythia have survived from this homestead. Check the trees and bushes carefully for warblers.

Beyond the observation-tower trailhead, continue for another 0.3 mile to a small clearing on the right side of the road. Park in the clearing and bird the edge of the woods and along the road. An Acadian Flycatcher spent the summer here in 1991.

Beyond the small clearing the road becomes rough. *You should continue only if your car has 4-wheel drive and adequate ground-clearance.* In 0.3 mile you will come to an area where the road starts to drop steeply down hill. There will be a steep uphill slope on the left side of the road. This area has been a hotspot for southern warblers. A few years ago, a singing male Kentucky Warbler was found here in mid-May. In May of 1994 a singing male Worm-eating Warbler was located on this same slope.

Continue for another 0.2 mile to a T in the road. Turn right and proceed for 0.5 mile to the trail leading to Boulder Field, an area of large boulders and cliffs. The trail is marked with white blazes leading from the road to Boulder Field. Listen for Winter Wren and Louisiana Waterthrush along this trail.

In 0.3 mile after Boulder Field you will come to a swamp on the left formed by Beavers. Look for Wood Ducks and Hooded Mergansers. In another 0.2 mile you will come to Round Pond on the right and the other end of the boulder trail on the left. Blue-gray Gnatcatchers and Cedar Waxwings have been known to nest on the edge of the pond. Watch for Turkey Vultures soaring overhead. The pond usually floods the road here, so you cannot continue. Even if not flooded, the road becomes too rough to drive beyond this point.

Turn around at Round Pond and backtrack to the T. Go straight across the top of the T (as opposed to turning left, which would return you to the tower). From the T proceed for 1.2 miles to the junction with Reservation Road. Along this stretch you will pass by a swamp and drive through a Red Pine forest. Continue to listen for warblers, vireos, and flycatchers. Turn right on Reservation Road and return 2.2 miles to State Route 107.

When you reach State Route 107, turn left to go south. In 3.0 miles you will come to the junction with State Route 27. Bear left to follow State Routes 107 and 27. In 4.0 miles, at a set of lights, turn right to stay on State Route 107 south. In 0.5 mile you will come to State Route 101. You can take State Route 101 west toward Manchester or east toward the seacoast.

Powwow Pond
to Powder House Pond

To
Rochester

To
Man-
chester

101

125

To
Newfields

To
Great
Bay

To
Stratham

85

Squamscott River

101

101

108

Brentwood

Powder
House
Pond

Exeter

To
Sea-
coast

111

High St

101C

boat
launch

Crawford
Ave

Exeter River

Lary Ln

P

power-line
swamp

108

Fire Pond

107

Kimball
Road

Drinkwater
Road

Kingston

111

Giles Rd

Great Brook

108

Great
Meadow

North Rd

150

East
Kingston

107

boat
launch

107A

pull-
off

108

108

107

Powwow River

Powwow
Pond

To
I-95
and
Seacoast

125

New Boston Rd

power-
line

To
Haverhill,
Massa-
chusetts

railroad

108

108

To
Haverhill,
Massa-
chusetts

North

0   Miles   2

F. POWWOW POND TO POWDER HOUSE POND

This trip takes you through the towns of Kingston, East Kingston, Kensington, and Exeter. A good time to bird this loop to find nesting species is late May, June, and July. Powwow Pond and Powder House Pond are also fruitful for migrating waterfowl in March to April and again in October to November. *Allow a half-day for this loop*, which has no facilities until you reach Exeter.

The starting-point is in Kingston at the northern of the two junctions of State Routes 107 and 125. From this junction take State Route 107 north for 0.7 mile to a swamp on the left side of the road. Pull off and park at the swamp, which is on the Little River. Look for Broad-winged Hawk, Belted Kingfisher, Northern Flicker, Eastern Wood-Pewee, Eastern Kingbird, Tufted Titmouse, White-breasted Nuthatch, Scarlet Tanager, and Red-winged Blackbird.

Powwow Pond

Return to the junction of State Routes 107 and 125 and head south on Route 125. Proceed for 1.5 miles and turn left (east) with Route 107 where it departs from Route 125 at the second set of lights. Take an immediate right (south) onto State Route 107A. In 0.8 mile you can see Powwow Pond on your right, by a marshy area on the edge of the road. There is room for a few cars to pull off here. Check for waterfowl in the marsh.

Proceed another 0.8 mile along State Route 107A and make a very hard right immediately after passing over the railroad tracks. Drive 100 yards on the dirt road down to the tracks and park off to the left. Walk southwest along the tracks for a quarter-mile to obtain a view of the pond. A spotting scope is useful here.

Migrant waterfowl species to look for include Pied-billed Grebe, Canada Goose, Green-winged Teal, American Black Duck, Mallard, Northern Pintail, Blue-winged Teal, Canvasback, Ring-necked Duck, Lesser Scaup, Bufflehead, Common Merganser, Ruddy Duck, and American Coot. You might also see an Osprey or a Bald Eagle during migration.

Return to State Route 107A and follow it southeast for 0.4 mile; turn right onto State Route 108. In 1.7 miles turn right onto New Boston Road. Go 2.4 miles to an unimproved boat-launch with room to park a few cars. Powwow Pond and the boat-launch will be on your right; the Powwow River will be to your left. Besides the prior access from the railroad track,

Northern Pintail
Georges Dremeaux

this is the only other clear vantage point of the pond, and an excellent point for scoping.

The active flow of the Powwow River—together with its far-southern location—makes this one of the first ponds in the state to provide open water in spring. Therefore, this is a productive spot to check in March because it often will concentrate the early spring waterfowl migrants.

This is also a good place to launch a canoe to explore both the pond and the river. The edge of the river supports many nesting species in June and July, including Broad-winged Hawk, Hairy Woodpecker, Eastern Phoebe, Eastern Kingbird, Bank and Barn Swallows, Tufted Titmouse, White-breasted Nuthatch, American Robin, Warbling and Red-eyed Vireos, Scarlet Tanager, and Song Sparrow.

Giles Road

Follow New Boston Road northwest for 0.3 mile beyond the boat-launch to the road's junction with State Route 125. Turn right on State Route 125, go 1.0 mile, and turn right at a set of lights at State Route 107. Proceed east on State Route 107 for 2.8 miles and turn left (north) on State Route 108 at the blinking yellow light. In 1.5 miles turn left on Giles Road and go 0.2 mile to where a tributary of Great Brook passes under the road. Park off to the side and bird from the edge of the road near the bridge. Look for Spotted Sandpiper (in migration), Eastern Wood-Pewee, Least and Great Crested Flycatchers, Veery, Wood Thrush, Red-eyed Vireo, Nashville (migrant), Chestnut-sided, and Black-throated Green Warblers, American Redstart, Ovenbird, Northern Cardinal, Rose-breasted Grosbeak, and Chipping Sparrow. This area consistently attracts birds that are usually found in more northerly locations, such as Winter Wren and White-throated Sparrow.

Sedge Meadow

Return to State Route 108, turn left, and go 1.0 mile, crossing into Kensington, and turn left onto Kimball Road. In 0.2 mile you will see a sedge meadow on your left. Park on the edge and walk along the road to bird for Marsh Wren, Warbling Vireo, Rose-breasted Grosbeak, Swamp Sparrow, Baltimore Oriole, and if you are lucky you may actually find a Sedge Wren here, as was the case in June 1994. Also, a Willow Flycatcher and an Alder Flycatcher have been observed here, engaged in a vocal duel from opposite sides of the same tall shrub!

Exeter River

Return to State Route 108, turn left, and continue heading north for 1.5 miles; then take a right on Lary Lane. In 0.4 mile the road ends in a cul-de-sac at a white concrete-block building. Park on the edge of the cul-de-sac and walk the path beside the building to reach the edge of the river. Follow the path leading off to the left which runs north along the west bank of the Exeter River.

As you walk along this path, watch the dense undergrowth on the opposite bank, which attracts migrating and nesting passerines. In particular, look for Yellow-bellied Sapsucker (migrant), Downy, Hairy, and Pileated Woodpeckers, Eastern Phoebe, Great Crested Flycatcher, Eastern Kingbird, Tufted Titmouse, Red-breasted and White-breasted Nuthatches, Gray Catbird, Chestnut-sided and Black-and-white Warblers, American Redstart, and Common Yellowthroat. Although it is most unusual in New Hampshire, a Prothonotary Warbler has been seen in this area. You might also find Green-winged Teal on the river during migration.

Return to State Route 108, turn right, and in 0.2 mile turn right onto Crawford Avenue. Follow Crawford for 0.5 mile and take a sharp right onto a gravel road that leads into a recreational park. There is a large parking area just before the baseball field. To reach the boat-launch, continue past the ballfield to the edge of the river, where it will be on your right. Here you can launch a canoe or other small boat and head south upriver (to the right when facing the river) for the best birding habitat.

As you canoe upriver, you will see several small channels on your left that do not go very far. You can canoe approximately one mile upriver until you reach a dead end at a large marsh. Be sure to listen for Alder and Willow Flycatchers. These two *Empidonax* flycatchers are best distinguished by song; listen for the *fee-BE-o* of the Alder and the *FITZ-bew* of the Willow. Watch overhead for Common Nighthawks that venture forth from the flat rooftops in Exeter to hunt for insects over the marsh.

Great Meadow

Return to State Route 108, turn left (south), and in 1.0 mile bear left at the fork in the road to go south on State Route 150. In 0.4 mile you will come to Great Meadow, a large marshy meadow on Great Brook. Park off to the edge on the right side of the road where the side road joins State Route 150 at the bend.

A scope is most useful here. As you look to the east (the left side of State Route 150), you can see a Great Blue Heron heronry in several large trees a few hundred yards away. The heronry was not occupied for the last couple of years, but it is hoped that the herons will return. The cattail marsh on the right side has nesting Virginia Rails and Soras. King Rail is also a remote possibility in this marsh during April and May. Look for such species as Glossy Ibis, Eastern Kingbird, Marsh Wren, Warbling Vireo, Song and Swamp Sparrows, and Red-winged Blackbird. In March, Rusty Blackbirds can be seen migrating through here. This is also another likely spot for Alder and Willow Flycatchers.

Drinkwater Road

Continue on State Route 150 for 0.9 mile and turn left onto North Road. In 0.9 mile bear left (north) onto Drinkwater Road (unmarked). This will take you into Exeter. In 0.8 mile pull off on the right by a pond with a fireplug. Look for migrant herons and waterfowl, plus Belted Kingfisher, Northern Cardinal, and Rose-breasted Grosbeak.

In another 0.7 mile there is a metal gate on the left side of the road with room to park a few cars off the road. This area is owned by Phillips

Exeter Academy and is posted with "no hunting" signs. Phillips Exeter Academy is a prestigious private high school, chartered in 1781. (Among relatively recent graduates are such luminaries as Arthur Schlesinger, Gore Vidal, John Irving, and Joyce Maynard.) The campus is located a short distance south of the center of Exeter.

Walk out the path beyond the gate, and you will enter a forest of large White Pines and hemlocks. This is prime habitat for Broad-winged Hawk, Hairy Woodpecker, Black-capped Chickadee, Red-breasted and White-breasted Nuthatches, Brown Creeper, Hermit Thrush, American Robin, Solitary Vireo, Nashville (migrant), Black-throated Green, and Pine Warblers, Ovenbird, and Scarlet Tanager. Northern Goshawks nest in these woods, and this is a regular spot to hear Barred Owls calling at night.

Continue on Drinkwater Road for an additional 0.3 mile to a small power-line crossing. Stop by the swamp on the right, under the power-line. Look for typical power-line birds such as Gray Catbird, Blue-winged, Yellow, Chestnut-sided, and Prairie Warblers, Indigo Bunting, Rufous-sided Towhee, and Field Sparrow.

Powder House Pond

Follow Drinkwater Road for another 0.6 mile to its intersection with State Route 101C (High Street) at a small traffic island. Turn left and go west 0.6 mile to State Route 108 in Exeter. Continue straight through the intersection to stay on High Street. In 0.1 mile turn right onto Pleasant Street and go uphill 0.1 mile to a stop-sign. Continue straight from the stop-sign for 0.2 mile to a T at Jady Hill Road. Turn left and follow Jady Hill Road down 150 yards to Powder House Pond.

Park along the edge of the pond, being careful not to block the roadway. This small pond can be a real hotspot, attracting an amazing variety of waterfowl during spring and fall migration. You can walk completely around the pond to obtain a close-up view of the waterfowl. On the west side, a raised dike separates the pond from the Squamscott River. On the east side you will find a small brick "powder house" (the pond's namesake) from the Revolutionary War. At the far end of the pond a path branches off and runs northward along the edge of the river for 0.2 mile. It is worthwhile following this path to see more of the river. There is another small pond to check at the end of the path.

Migrants to look for here include Pied-billed Grebe; Double-crested Cormorant; Canada Goose; Green-winged Teal; American Black Duck; Mallard; Northern Pintail; Blue-winged Teal; Northern Shoveler; Gadwall; American Wigeon; Canvasback; Redhead (rare); Ring-necked Duck; Lesser Scaup; Common Goldeneye; Hooded, Common, and Red-breasted Mergansers; Ruddy Duck (rare); American Coot; Common Snipe; Chimney Swift; Tree, Cliff, and Barn Swallows; American Tree and Swamp Sparrows; and Red-winged Blackbird. A Yellow-crowned Night-Heron has been seen here in June.

The Squamscott River (the tidal extension of the Exeter River) flows from Exeter north to Great Bay. During shorebird migration check along the edge of the river at low tide for a variety of shorebirds. (High tide for this tidal river is approximately three hours after the seacoast—Boston—high tide.) You should also find Ring-billed, Herring, and Great Black-backed Gulls on the river. Northern Rough-winged Swallows nest in the stone wall on the opposite (west) side of the river.

Be sure to check carefully in the White Pines near the powder house. During late summer and fall, Black-crowned Night-Herons roost high up in these pine trees.

Return to Pleasant Street, turn right, and go 0.3 mile back to State Route 108 (High Street). Turn left and backtrack for 0.1 mile to the traffic-light. Turn left to follow State Route 108 north. Along this stretch of State Route 108 in Exeter you will find stores, gas stations, motels, and restaurants.

Powder House Pond, waterfowl hotspot.

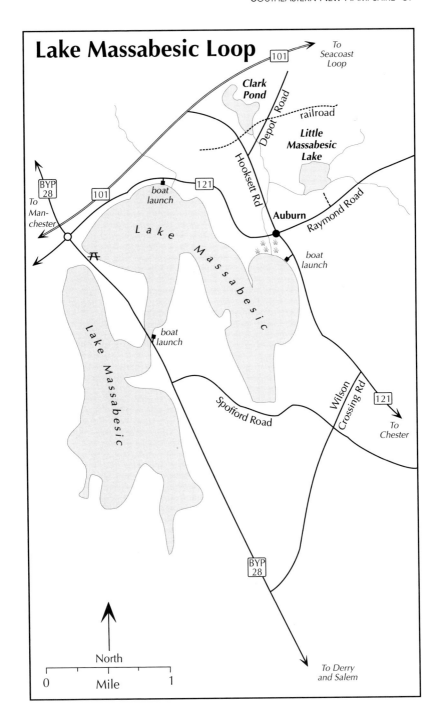

Lake Massabesic Loop

101 To Seacoast Loop

Clark Pond

Depot Road

railroad

Little Massabesic Lake

Hooksett Rd

BYP 28

101

121

boat launch

To Man-chester

L a k e

Auburn

Raymond Road

M a s s a b e s i c

boat launch

boat launch

L a k e   M a s s a b e s i c

Wilson Crossing Rd

121

To Chester

Spofford Road

BYP 28

North

0   Mile   1

To Derry and Salem

G. LAKE MASSABESIC LOOP

Because of its status as the Manchester city reservoir, Lake Massabesic is a clean, clear lake with an undeveloped shoreline. The surface of the lake encompasses 2,500 acres, placing it among the largest lakes in southern New Hampshire. Lake Massabesic is one of the southernmost nesting locations for Common Loon in the state. Boating is permitted, although swimming, wading, and water-skiing are not.

At many points around the lake you can easily scan for waterfowl from the edge of the road. At other locations, large sections of woods isolate the lake from the road. There are numerous access roads leading to the lake through these wooded areas. These woods roads are barricaded to motor vehicles, but you can park your car at the gate and walk along them. All traveler services can be found in Manchester. This area provides fruitful birding in spring, summer, and fall. A spotting scope is useful for this trip, *which should take a half-day.*

The starting-point for this loop around Lake Massabesic is the traffic rotary at the junction of State Route 121 and State Route 28 By-pass, at the northwest corner of the lake. You will find gas stations and convenience markets at the rotary. The loop around the lake is done in a clockwise direction, keeping the lake on your right, to make it easier to pull off and bird from the edge of the road.

Hooded Mergansers
Shawneen E. Finnegan

From the rotary, drive east on State Route 121 for 1.0 mile. Pull off to the edge of the road anywhere in the next 0.2 mile to scan the lake for migrating Pied-billed Grebe, Canada Goose, American Black Duck, Mallard, Ring-necked Duck, Common Goldeneye, Bufflehead, and Hooded and Common Mergansers. Also look for summer-resident Common Loon and Great Black-backed and Herring Gulls. At this point (1.2 miles from the rotary) there is a public boat-launch.

From the boat-launch, continue on State Route 121 as it veers away from the shoreline, enters a wooded area, and passes by three access roads to the lake. You will see them at the 0.4-, 0.6-, and 1.25-mile marks from the boat-launch. You can stop at any of these and take a short easy walk through the woods to the lake. Bird species to expect include Ruffed Grouse, Eastern Kingbird, Black-capped Chickadee, Red-breasted and White-breasted Nuthatches, Hermit Thrush, Gray Catbird, Red-eyed Vireo, Common Yellowthroat, Song Sparrow, Red-winged Blackbird, and Common Grackle.

Little Massabesic Lake

At the 1.5-mile mark from the boat-launch you will come to a 4-way intersection. Go straight across the intersection onto Raymond Road (unmarked). Follow this road for 0.7 mile (at the 0.4-mile mark it becomes gravel) to a gate on the left. There is room to park a few cars on the edge of the road. *Do not block the gate.* Walk out the road beyond the gate for a quarter-mile to Little Massabesic Lake. During spring and fall look for migrant species such as American Black Duck, Common Merganser, Osprey, Golden-crowned Kinglet, and Pine Siskin.

Clark Pond

Return to the 4-way intersection, turn right onto Hooksett Road, go 0.9 mile, and turn right onto Depot Road. In 0.25 mile pull off on the left in a sandy parking area next to a small pond. Walk around the right side of the small pond and go 75 yards to the railroad bed. Turn left and walk along the railroad bed for 50 yards to a bridge over the stream. From the bridge there is a clear view of Clark Pond. This is worth checking during spring and fall for migrating waterfowl. During spring and summer it may be worth your while to walk down the railroad bed in search of passerines.

Return to Massabesic Lake

Return to State Route 121 at the 4-way intersection. Go straight through the intersection to take State Route 121 south. In 0.1 mile pull off on the right near a stone monument. Scan the marshy area along the stream that drains into Lake Massabesic. During April's ice break-up this inlet provides the first open water on the Lake, producing an immediate attraction for waterfowl. This is a typical spot for Pied-billed Grebe, Green-winged Teal, Lesser Scaup, Bufflehead, and Hooded Merganser. Later in migration look for American Bittern, Great Egret, Virginia Rail, and Belted Kingfisher.

There is an immense Beaver lodge in the middle of the marshy area. At dawn or dusk you may see a Beaver on patrol. This area also attracts River Otter, especially in spring.

Continue along State Route 121 for another 0.1 mile to a gravel parking lot and boat-launch on the right. From this parking lot you have a view of the marsh to the right and the lake to the left. As you leave the parking lot, turn right to continue south on State Route 121. Drive slowly

Common Loons
Shawneen E. Finnegan

along this section and watch for Common Loons, which frequent this edge of the lake. The road soon climbs up a hill and veers away from the lake.

After driving 1.5 miles from the parking lot and boat-launch, turn right onto Wilson Crossing Road and proceed 0.7 mile to a 4-way intersection. Turn right onto Spofford Road and go 1.9 miles to State Route 28 By-pass. Turn right and go north for 0.5 mile to another boat-launch on the right. Stop here and look for Common Loon. If the boat-launch area is busy, you can continue just beyond the bridge and pull off on the right for a good viewing-site. In 0.2 mile from the boat-launch there is another gated woods road on the right. This is a great spot to find wild blueberries and huckleberries in late July and early August.

From the boat-launch, continue north on State Route 28 By-pass for 0.8 mile to a park on the right, just before the rotary. The park is open from 8 am to 8 pm and has picnic tables, but no restrooms. As you leave the park, turn right and you will immediately reach the rotary where this loop started.

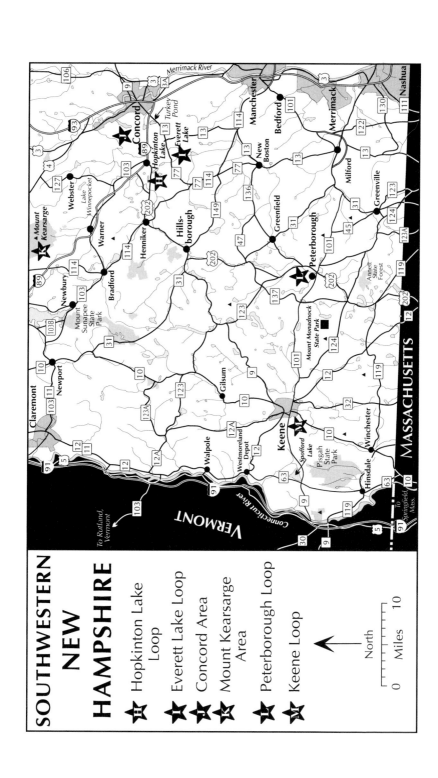

Chapter 2:

SOUTHWESTERN NEW HAMPSHIRE

This section is defined by a line running from the Tilton/Franklin area south along Interstate 93 to the Massachusetts boundary, and another line from the Tilton/Franklin area west to Vermont. As you head west, the state becomes much more sparsely populated, and the Monadnock Mountains rise up in the distance to greet you. Southwestern New Hampshire has several mountains in the 2,000- to 3,000-foot range. During the fall foliage season this section of the state is particularly beautiful. It also has the advantage of not being as crowded with tourists as the White Mountains of central New Hampshire.

Black-throated Blue Warbler
Barry W. Van Dusen

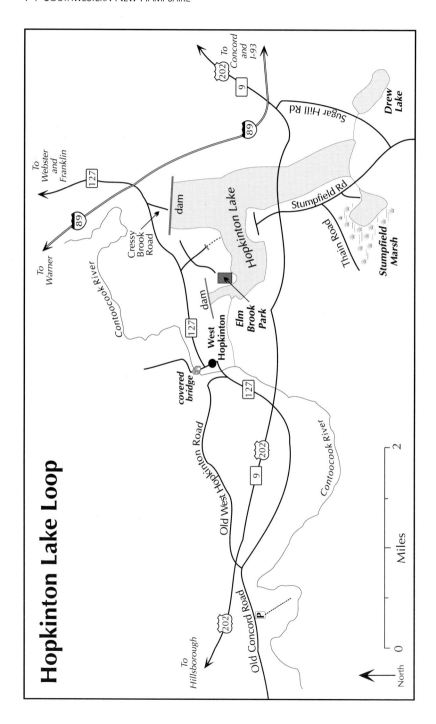

Hopkinton Lake Loop

H. HOPKINTON LAKE LOOP

During the early 1960s the United States Army Corps of Engineers built a series of dams in the towns of Hopkinton, Weare, and Dunbarton to control flooding in the Merrimack River Valley. Besides the resulting Hopkinton and Everett Lakes, there are also marshes, swamps, and upland woodlands, providing a variety of habitats. Spring and fall are productive seasons in which to visit for waterfowl migration. May, June, and July are the months to observe nesting birds. *This loop requires a half-day.* All traveler services are available in nearby Concord.

To reach this area follow Interstate 89 west from Interstate 93, just south of Concord. Take Exit 5 off I-89 to U.S. Highway 202 west. Follow 202 for 1.2 miles and turn left onto Stumpfield Road. Go 0.5 mile and turn right onto Thain Road (unmarked dirt road) just before a red house. In 0.2 mile stop at the swamp on the right side of the road. Look for Sharp-shinned Hawk, Eastern Wood-Pewee, Eastern Phoebe, Eastern Kingbird, Red-breasted and White-breasted Nuthatches, Brown Creeper, Solitary and Red-eyed Vireos, Yellow-rumped and Palm (migrant) Warblers, and Song Sparrow.

Stumpfield Marsh

Turn around here and return to Stumpfield Road. As you drive along Stumpfield Road, watch and listen for Northern Bobwhites, which are occasionally found in this area. (Any Northern Bobwhites that you encounter in New Hampshire are probably released gamebirds.) Turn right and continue down Stumpfield Road for 0.2 mile to a small (unmarked) dirt road on the right. There is a yellow gate at the entrance to this road, which leads 0.2 mile to Stumpfield Marsh. This road drops off sharply for the first 100 feet and then levels out. The road is rough, so if your car does not have plenty of ground clearance you may want to park on the edge of Stumpfield Road and walk the short distance to the marsh.

Where the road ends at the marsh there is plenty of room to park. In summer, white and yellow water-lilies bloom, as well as Pickerelweed. There is a fine view of a Great Blue Heron colony with about two dozen nests, and several Wood Duck boxes. This marsh has a large expanse of open water and is a nice spot to launch a canoe. From the boat-launch, if you paddle to the left you can follow the stream under the road to reach Elm Brook Marsh, a large open wetland.

Other birds to look for in summer include Turkey Vulture, Virginia Rail, Belted Kingfisher, Downy, Hairy, and Pileated Woodpeckers, Northern Flicker, Eastern Wood-Pewee, Great Crested Flycatcher, Tree, Northern Rough-winged, Cliff, and Barn Swallows, Tufted Titmouse, Red-breasted and White-breasted Nuthatches, Hermit Thrush, Yellow-rumped Warbler, Rufous-sided Towhee, Song Sparrow, and Red-winged Blackbird. In migration look for Pied-billed Grebe, Double-crested Cormorant, Ring-necked Duck, Lesser Scaup, Common Merganser, Osprey, Golden-crowned Kinglet, Palm Warbler, and Swamp Sparrow.

Drew Lake

Return to Stumpfield Road, turn right, go 0.7 mile, and take a sharp left onto Sugar Hill Road (unmarked). Proceed 0.4 mile to Drew Lake, which will be on your right. There is a convenient place to launch a canoe or small boat by the dam. You can bird the path on the right, just before the dam, which skirts the lake, or take the old woods road on the left across from the path. You can also bird the brushy area on the opposite side of the road from the lake. Look here for Gray Catbird, Red-eyed Vireo, Yellow Warbler, Common Yellowthroat, Song Sparrow, Red-winged Blackbird, and American Goldfinch.

Elm Brook Pool

Continue up Sugar Hill Road for 1.0 mile to U.S. Highway 202. Loop around to go west on U.S. Highway 202 again (follow the sign toward Henniker) for 1.0 mile and turn right at the signs directing you to Elm Brook Pool and boat-launch (opposite Stumpfield Road). This road is paved but nevertheless is rather rough. In 0.3 mile turn left at the crossroads and go 0.2 mile to the boat-launch and parking lot. This is a popular spot with fishermen. It also provides a convenient point from which to scope the lake for migrating waterfowl. Look for Pied-billed, Horned, and Red-necked (fall) Grebes, Mallard, Northern Pintail, Ring-necked Duck, Lesser Scaup, White-winged Scoter, Hooded and Red-breasted Mergansers, Osprey, and Belted Kingfisher.

Return to the crossroads and continue straight across for 0.2 mile to where the road ends. This is another good vantage point from which to scope for migrating waterfowl.

Sparrow field with Pat's Peak in the background.

Old Concord Road

Return to U.S. Highway 202 and turn right to continue heading west. In 4.0 miles turn left at the blinking yellow light at the sign for Old West Hopkinton Road. Take an immediate right at the T onto Old Concord Road (unmarked). Follow this road for 0.6 mile to a dirt road leading through the field on the left. (The dirt road will be at the end of a line of granite posts.) Pull in on the left at the mouth of the dirt road and park by the sign reading "No motorized vehicles beyond this point." (Do not block the road. Tractors use it to access the fields. Walk out the dirt road through the field to bird for Vesper, Savannah, and Grasshopper Sparrows, Bobolink, and Eastern Meadowlark. *Please stay on the road; do not trespass onto the hay crops.* American Kestrels have nested in a dead tree on the west end of the field. Listen for Black-billed Cuckoo, plus Alder and Willow Flycatchers, calling from the overgrown fields on the opposite side of the road.

Elm Brook Park

Return to U.S. Highway 202 and turn right. Backtrack 1.7 miles east and turn left at the blinking yellow light onto State Route 127. In 0.7 mile bear right to stay on State Route 127 and drive across the dam. Another 0.3 mile will bring you to a fork in the road near a covered bridge which crosses the Contoocook River. Bear right before the bridge, to continue on State Route 127. Proceed for 1.0 mile and bear right at the signs to Elm Brook Park and Recreation Area. In 0.1 mile you will come to a 4-way junction, although the intersection is somewhat askew.

Take a shallow right to continue straight across the intersection on a dirt road, with a sign indicating that this is a dead end. It is also a rough road, so if your vehicle does not have adequate ground clearance you may want to skip this road. Just beyond 0.3 mile you will reach a barricade of large boulders. There is an old road which cuts across the road that you are on. It is barred by gates on both sides, but you can park along the edge and walk in either direction to look for woodland birds. Wild Turkeys are sometimes seen in this area. The Hopkinton Lake Loop and the Everett Lake Loop (the following section) are the best areas in New Hampshire in which to find a Wild Turkey.

You can walk along the main dirt road for about another 0.1 mile to the edge of the water. You will find a large open grassy area. There is a sign indicating that this was the original site of Stumpfield Cemetery, which was moved in 1961. You should expect to find birds here similar to those listed previously under Elm Brook Pool.

If it is time for your picnic lunch or if you need a restroom, return to the 4-way intersection, turn left, and proceed 0.2 mile to the entrance booth (no fee) to Elm Brook Park. Stop and ask for a map which shows the entire Hopkinton/Everett Lake area, including details of the park. This delightful park is run by the United States Army Corps of Engineers and offers picnic tables, cooking grills, restrooms, a swimming area, and a nature trail. During summer the park is open from 9 am to 8 pm.

If you are sharp, you may find a Northern Bobwhite or a Savannah Sparrow in the grassy areas. During fall migration a few American Golden-Plovers have been seen in the fields. The half-mile nature trail, through a predominantly White Pine forest, has common birds such as Black-capped Chickadee, American Robin, Gray Catbird, Yellow Warbler, Common Yellowthroat, Scarlet Tanager, and Song Sparrow. A guide to the trail is available at the trailhead. Flora to look for along the trail include Bunchberry, Canada Mayflower, Partridgeberry, and ferns. From stop number 4 you will have a view of a marshy area on the edge of Hopkinton Lake. In May 1993 a Black Tern was seen migrating over the lake.

Return to State Route 127, turn right, go 0.8 mile, and turn right onto Cressy Brook Road. Follow this road to a dead end in 0.2 mile. Park at the barricade and walk up the old road to the right. If the gate is closed, you can take the short trail around it through the woods. Follow the old road for a quarter-mile to the edge of the dike. Turn left and walk along the top of the dike. There is a clear view of the lake below. A spotting scope is useful to scan for waterfowl.

Return to State Route 127, turn right, and go 0.2 mile to Exit 6 of Interstate 89. This is the conclusion of this loop. You can access Interstate 89 here to go north or south.

American Golden-Plover
Georges Dremeaux

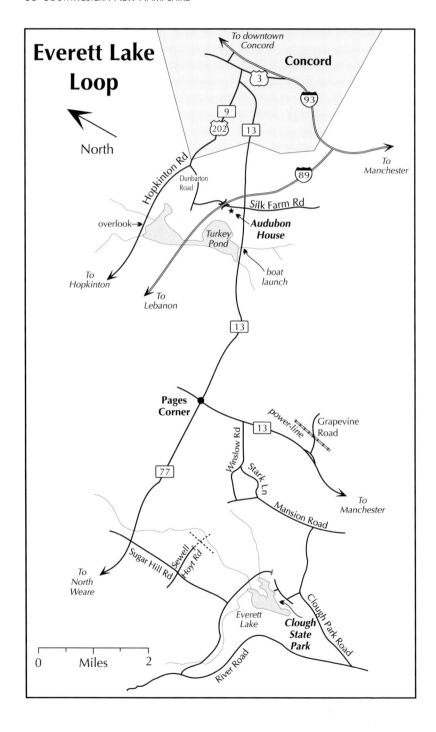

Everett Lake Loop

North

Concord

To downtown
Concord

3

93

9

202

13

89

To
Manchester

Hopkinton Rd

Dunbarton
Road

Silk Farm Rd

Audubon
House

overlook→

Turkey
Pond

To
Hopkinton

boat
launch

To
Lebanon

13

Pages
Corner

power-line

Grapevine
Road

13

Winslow Rd

Stark Ln

77

Mansion Road

To
Manchester

Sugar Hill Rd

Sewell

Hoyt Rd

To
North
Weare

Everett
Lake

Clough
State
Park

Clough Park Road

River Road

0   Miles   2

I. EVERETT LAKE LOOP

Everett Lake is also part of the United States Army Corps of Engineers flood-control project. All traveler services are available in nearby Concord. Like the Hopkinton Lake Loop, this area provides worthwhile birding in spring, summer, and fall. *Allow a half-day for this loop.*

Turkey Pond

To reach this area follow Interstate 89 west from Interstate 93, just south of Concord. Take Exit 2 off Interstate 89 and follow State Route 13 south for 0.3 mile. Turn right onto Silk Farm Road and go 0.2 mile to the headquarters of the independent Audubon Society of New Hampshire. The headquarters is open Monday through Saturday from 9 am to 5 pm, Sunday 1 pm to 5 pm, and provides a nature store, modest library, and restrooms.

Because of its proximity to Audubon House, Turkey Pond is one of the most heavily birded spots in the state. Thus, the list of species recorded here is large and varied. You should not expect to see the majority of these species on any one visit, but they have all occurred here.

From Audubon House the yellow trail leads out to Turkey Pond. During spring and fall migrations, look for Pied-billed and Horned Grebes, Double-crested Cormorant, Green-winged and Blue-winged Teals, American Black Duck, American Wigeon, Ring-necked Duck, White-winged Scoter, American Coot, and Swamp Sparrow. Nesting season should produce Eastern Wood-Pewee and Red-breasted and White-breasted Nuthatches. During August and September look for American Golden-Plover, Spotted, Baird's, Pectoral, and Stilt Sandpipers, Dunlin, Short-billed Dowitcher, American Pipit, and thousands of Red-winged Blackbirds.

To find another vantage point for Turkey Pond, turn left as you leave Audubon House and go 0.8 mile to a T at Dunbarton Road. Turn right and go 0.75 mile to U.S. Highway 202 (also called Hopkinton Road). Turn left onto U.S. Highway 202 and go 1.4 miles to a pull-off on the right from which you can see Little Turkey Pond on the left.

Return to State Route 13 and continue heading south; in 0.7 mile you will come to a gravel parking area on the left side of the road, with Turkey Pond on the right. You can launch a canoe or other small craft on the left side, by the bridge, and proceed under the bridge and out onto Turkey Pond.

Sugar Hill Road

Resume your course south on State Route 13 for 2.7 miles to a power-line crossing. You can park off to the edge of the road and walk out on the power-line road to look for Gray Catbird, Chestnut-sided and Prairie Warblers, Common Yellowthroat, Rufous-sided Towhee, and Field Sparrow. Listen for Veery and Hermit Thrush in the adjacent woods.

After the power-line, another 0.3 mile on State Route 13 will bring you to a 4-way intersection at Pages Corner. Continue straight through the intersection to follow State Route 77 heading west. In 2.9 miles (having passed into the township of Weare) go left at a 4-way intersection onto Sugar Hill Road (not marked). Follow Sugar Hill Road for 1.0 mile and turn left at a 4-way intersection onto Sewell Hoyt Road (dirt). Go 0.6 mile and park by the barricade. Walk 100 yards straight in beyond the barricade on the old road to a 4-way junction. These old roads are used by motor bikes and snowmobiles, but they also provide an excellent place to walk while you look and listen for birds.

The habitat in this area is productive for nesting wood warblers and other passerines. Look for Red-breasted Nuthatch, Solitary and Red-eyed Vireos, Northern Parula, Nashville (migrant), Black-throated Green, Pine, Black-and-white, and Canada Warblers, Ovenbird, and American Goldfinch. Listen for the high-pitched virtuoso trills of the tiny Winter Wren, more easily heard than seen. You may develop the impression that you are in the north country as you hear the upward spirals of the Hermit Thrush and listen to the White-throated Sparrow as it tells of *Sweet Canada, Canada, Canada.* If you are lucky, you may even see a Wild Turkey strutting along.

Piscataquog River

Return to Sugar Hill Road and turn left to continue heading south. In 1.2 miles the pavement ends at a T in the road. Turn left and proceed for 0.4 mile to a pull-off on the right overlooking a swamp in the distance. Look around carefully in this area and you will see old cellar-holes and driveways where homes were once located before the area was taken over for the flood-control project. You will find an interesting variety of plant life too, including wild roses, Day-lilies, Milkweed, Cow (or Blue) Vetch, Thimbleberries, Yarrow, and grapevines. These serve to attract various bird species.

Along the section between Sugar Hill Road and the overlook, watch for Sharp-shinned, Broad-winged, and Red-tailed Hawks, American Kestrel, Belted Kingfisher, Northern Flicker, Willow and Least Flycatchers, Eastern Phoebe, Eastern Kingbird, Red-breasted and White-breasted Nuthatches, Brown Creeper, Ruby-crowned Kinglet (migrant), American Robin, Gray Catbird, Rufous-sided Towhee, and Field and Song Sparrows. This a reliable spot for Blue-gray Gnatcatcher and Eastern Bluebird.

Continue for another 0.3 mile and park by a path leading up the hill to the right. A short walk up over this rise will give you an excellent view of the swamp from the high overlook. Scan for waterfowl. During summer the swamp displays white Fragrant Water-lily and yellow Spatterdock or Pond-lily and Pickerelweed. Here in the spring of 1995 a Yellow-throated Warbler was found singing in the pine trees; there had been less than a dozen previous state records for this warbler. This illustrates the potential that this interesting area has for attracting rarities. In 0.1 mile after this path look for Northern Rough-winged Swallows nesting under the bridge that crosses the stream. During migration scan along the shore of the stream for Solitary Sandpiper.

Another 0.2 mile from the bridge will bring you to a gate blocking the road at the back side of Clough State Park. You cannot enter the park from this point, but the area just outside the gate is well worth birding. The brushy area growing in with saplings, on the left side of the road just before the gate, is usually reliable for nesting Black-billed Cuckoo, Alder Flycatcher, and House Wren. A Yellow-billed Cuckoo is not out of the question here.

Return to the T at the foot of Sugar Hill Road and continue straight past Sugar Hill Road to go out the other side of the T. You are now heading west. In the next few miles there are several convenient stops to make along the edge of the Piscataquog (pis-CAT-uh-kwog) River on your left. Along this stretch by the river look for Yellow-bellied Sapsucker, Hairy Woodpecker, Black-capped Chickadee, Hermit Thrush, Solitary, Yellow-throated, and Warbling Vireos, Yellow, Chestnut-sided, Pine, and Black-and-white Warblers, American Redstart, Ovenbird, Louisiana Waterthrush, Common Yellowthroat, Rose-breasted Grosbeak, Indigo Bunting, and Chipping and White-throated Sparrows.

The first stop is a nice pull-off on the left in 0.2 mile (past Sugar Hill Road) that overlooks the river. Continue for another 0.3 mile and turn left onto a small dirt road, bearing left again to follow the road along the river for 0.1 mile to where it ends in a loop. Check along the riverbank for birds. The heavy undergrowth of grapevines along the river provides desirable cover for small passerines. You will be up higher than the opposite bank of the river, giving you great positioning to look down upon the birds.

Return to the main dirt road and turn left to continue heading west. In 0.1 mile turn left on another dirt side-road. This soon becomes too rough to drive. Park and walk 200 yards to the edge of the river. This is a nice spot for a picnic. Resume your course west and in 0.1 mile pull off and park on the left by a pair of dirt roads. Walk out the left road by the sign indicating "No Wheeled Vehicles." Going 100 yards out this road, you will come to a small meadow on your left. In summer look here for Ring-necked Pheasant, Tree Swallow, Bobolink, and Eastern Meadowlark.

Resume driving west for another 0.3 mile, at which point you will come to a small grassy clearing on your right. Stop at the clearing and pish for Black-capped Chickadees and warblers. Continue for another 0.2 mile, crossing over a small bridge spanning the river. Just past the bridge, pull off on the right at the mouth of an old woods road. There is a swamp on the opposite side of the road with a short trail through the woods to the swamp's edge. You will find another vantage point of the same swamp in another 0.2 mile down the road, where the road abuts the edge of a cattail marsh. In summer look for Great Blue Heron, Virginia Rail, and Eastern Phoebe.

Clough State Park

Continue another 0.4 mile to a paved road. Turn left onto River Road, go 4.2 miles, and take a sharp left onto Clough Park Road. In 2.1 miles turn left into Clough State Park just before the Weare/Dunbarton town line. A small fee is collected at the entrance booth for each person over 12 years of age. Park facilities include picnic tables, cooking grills, restrooms, drinking water, a swimming beach with life guards, and a boat-launch. The park is open from 9 am to 7:30 pm from Memorial Day through Labor Day.

From the entrance, take your first right and then your first left to reach the boat-launch. No gasoline engines are allowed, but electric motors are permitted. Of course, you can also paddle or row,$Icanoe. As you leave the boat-ramp, turn left onto the service road and proceed to the gate at the western edge of the park. (This is the same gate that you approached from the other side off Sugar Hill Road.) Birds found in the park include Eastern Phoebe, Red-breasted Nuthatch, Wood Thrush, American Robin, Gray Catbird, and Song Sparrow.

When you leave the park, turn left and go 1.2 miles to a T. Turn left onto Mansion Road (unmarked). Follow this for another 1.3 miles and bear right onto Stark Lane (which later becomes Winslow Road). In 1.3

miles pull off to the side of the road, just before or after the guard rail, where there is a marsh on both sides. During summer look for Broad-winged Hawk, Killdeer, Eastern Phoebe, Barn Swallow, and American Robin. During August and September look for migrating shorebirds on the mudflats.

At the end of the marsh the road comes to a T. Turn right onto Route 13 and go 1.3 miles to turn left onto Burnham Road. In 0.1 mile turn left again onto Grapevine Road. Proceed 0.4 mile and park off to the edge of the road at the power-line crossing. Walk out the power-line right-of-way on the left side of the road for a spectacular view. The power-line runs north and south, and on a clear day you can see north to the White Mountains.

You should find the typical species that power-lines attract: Gray Catbird, Chestnut-sided and Prairie Warblers, Common Yellowthroat, Rufous-sided Towhee, and Field Sparrow. You may also hear Veery, Hermit Thrush, and Red-eyed Vireo in the adjacent woods. Wild Turkeys have been seen in this area. If conditions are favorable in fall, with a north or a northwest wind, this can be a rewarding hawk-watching location, too.

Return to State Route 13 and turn right to go north. In 2.2 miles you will come to the 4-way intersection at Pages Corner. Turn right to stay on State Route 13 for another 3.8 miles to return to Interstate 89.

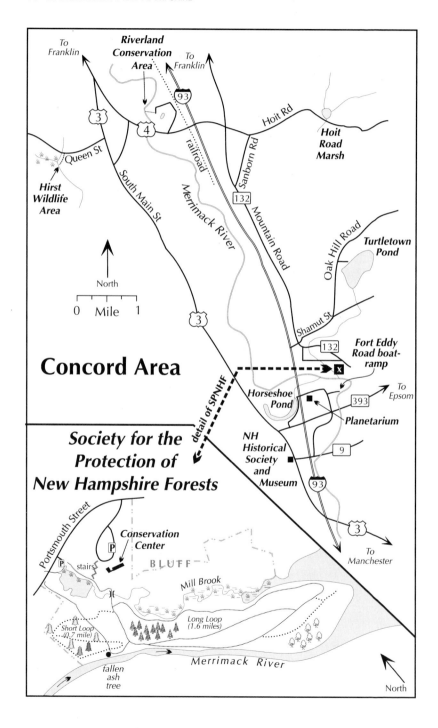

To Franklin

Riverland Conservation Area

To Franklin

93

Hoit Rd

Hoit Road Marsh

3

4

Queen St

Railroad

Sanborn Rd

132

Hirst Wildlife Area

South Main St

Merrimack River

Mountain Road

Oak Hill Road

Turtletown Pond

North

0   Mile   1

3

Shamut St

132

Fort Eddy Road boat-ramp

Concord Area

X

detail of SPNHF

Horseshoe Pond

393

To Epsom

Planetarium

Society for the Protection of New Hampshire Forests

NH Historical Society and Museum

9

93

3

To Manchester

Portsmouth Street

Conservation Center

P

stairs

BLUFF

Mill Brook

P

Long Loop (1.6 miles)

Short Loop (0.7 mile)

Merrimack River

fallen ash tree

North

J. CONCORD AREA

This trip embraces a collection of quick stops in the Concord area *which will take a half-day*. Spring, summer, and fall are rewarding seasons to bird the area. All traveler services are available in the city of Concord. The famous "Concord Coach", used by Wells Fargo in opening the American frontier, was designed in Concord, New Hampshire. The New Hampshire Historical Society and Museum (603/225-3381), located at 30 Park Street in Concord, displays a Concord Coach as well as other historical items. Also of interest is the headquarters of the Society for the Protection of New Hampshire Forests.

For tourist information on the Concord area write or call:

- Greater Concord Chamber of Commerce
  244 North Main Street
  Concord, NH 03301
  603/224-2508

Fort Eddy Road Boat-Ramp

From Interstate 93 in Concord, take Exit 15E, follow Interstate 393 east for 0.2 mile, and take Exit 1 for Fort Eddy Road. Turn left at the end of the ramp to follow Fort Eddy Road north (toward the Planetarium and the New Hampshire Technical Institute) for 0.4 mile, and turn right onto an unmarked gravel road. Drive 0.1 mile to a parking area and paved boat-launch at the edge of the Merrimack River. During waterfowl migration this can be a productive spot. This location is also worth a stop during winter if the river is not frozen. Check the nearby fields for migrant sparrows, Horned Larks, and Snow Buntings.

If you have time while in the Concord area, you may want to pay a visit to the Planetarium, which features exhibits and a planetarium show. Reservations are recommended for the show and are available by calling 603/271-STAR, Monday through Saturday from 9 am to 4 pm.

Horseshoe Pond

From the boat-ramp, turn right and continue on Fort Eddy Road. Turn right in 0.1 mile to stay on Fort Eddy Road, go a total of 0.7 mile, passing over Interstate 93, until you come to a T at Commercial Street. Turn left, and as you proceed along Commercial Street you will see Horseshoe Pond on your right. Stop anywhere that affords you a view of the pond

American Woodcock
Georges Dremeaux

through the trees that border the road. This is a regular spot for waterfowl migrants, including Pied-billed and Horned Grebes, Canada Goose, American Black Duck, Mallard, Northern Shoveler, Gadwall, American Wigeon, Ring-necked Duck, and Bufflehead. Other migrants to look for are Common Snipe and American Woodcock.

After a total of 0.5 mile on Commercial Street turn left onto South Commercial Street (unmarked) and proceed 0.2 mile to a set of lights. Turn left and go 0.2 mile to Interstate 93 north. To visit the Society for the Protection of New Hampshire Forests and Turtletown Pond, take Interstate 93 north for 1.2 miles.

Society for the Protection of New Hampshire Forests

Exit Interstate 93 at Exit 16. From the end of the exit ramp bear right to go east for 0.1 mile to a disjoint 4-way intersection with State Route 132. From the junction of State Route 132 and Shamut Street, turn right onto 132, then immediately bear left at the fork onto East Side Drive and continue up hill following the signs to the conservation center. In 0.7 mile turn right onto Portsmouth Street, proceed for 0.2 mile, turning left into the conservation center at the headquarters of the Society for the Protection of New Hampshire Forests. This property encompasses 95 acres of land along the edge of the Merrimack River.

The center is open from 8:30 am to 5 pm Monday through Friday (54 Portsmouth Street, Concord, NH 03301; 603/224-9945). The trails are open seven days a week from dawn to dusk. Perched atop a bluff, the

American Wigeons
Barry W. Van Dusen

center provides a commanding view of the Merrimack River floodplain. The center employs several innovative passive solar-heating techniques which you may study by taking a self-guided tour of the facility.

The Society for the Protection of New Hampshire Forests, often just called "the Forest Society," was founded in 1901. A private, non-profit organization, it is one of the largest conservation groups in the state. Its programs cover a combination of land management, land protection, education, and legislation.

You may reach the trails by taking the long set of zig-zag stairs from just outside the building. Another alternative is to continue down Portsmouth Street for another 0.2 mile beyond the center to the parking lot on the left at the trailhead.

Look for migrant Solitary Sandpiper, Yellow-bellied Flycatcher, and warblers such as Tennessee, Magnolia, Blackburnian, and Northern Parula.

During summer you should find nesting Black-billed Cuckoo, Least and Great Crested Flycatchers, Eastern Kingbird, Veery, Gray Catbird, Solitary Vireo, Blue-winged, Pine, Prairie, and Black-and-white Warblers, American Redstart, and Rose-breasted Grosbeak. Belted Kingfishers and Bank Swallows nest in the sandy banks along the river.

Turtletown Pond

Return to the junction of State Route 132 and Shamut Street. Turn right onto Shamut Street and follow it for 0.7 mile. Bear left at the fork onto Oak Hill Road. In 0.8 mile turn right at the sign for "Turtletown Pond Boat Access Facility." There is a boat-launch and a paved parking area providing a clear view of the pond. The pond can be productive for the usual migrating waterfowl: Common Loon, Pied-billed and Red-necked Grebes, Canada Goose, Ring-necked Duck, Bufflehead, and Hooded and Common Mergansers. You may also find Bank Swallows here.

Hoit Road Marsh

From Turtletown Pond return to the junction with State Route 132 (Mountain Road) and turn right to go north on State Route 132. In 2.9 miles turn right onto Sanborn Road, proceed for 0.9 mile, and turn right onto Hoit Road. Follow Hoit Road for 1.5 miles to Hoit Road Marsh. There is a parking area and boat-launch on the left and additional parking on the right side of the road. During nesting season look for Wood Duck and Red-winged Blackbird. This can also be a good spot during waterfowl migration.

Riverland Conservation Area

From Hoit Road Marsh return on Hoit Road and proceed for 2.9 miles, going past Sanborn Road, over Interstate 93, onto U.S. Highway 4, turning right at the brown sign for Riverland Conservation Area. (There is a street sign at this road for Shoe String and Old Boyce Roads.) Immediately after turning right, stay left at the fork. In 0.5 mile the road changes from paved to gravel and veers left to parallel the railroad tracks. Continue for another 0.2 mile and turn left where there is a small red sign on a telephone pole reading "park closes at sunset." In 0.3 mile turn left again at another red sign reading the same, and drive through the gate to the parking area.

There you will notice a sign with park rules and a mailbox with trail guides. At the left end of the parking area there is a small pond whose shores should be checked for Green Heron, Least Flycatcher, and migrant warblers. Great Egret has been seen here in late summer. Check around the parking area for Brown Thrasher and Rose-breasted Grosbeak. From the right end of the parking area, beyond a metal gate, a grassy path leads a quarter-mile to the Merrimack River. Birds to look for along this path include Tree and Bank Swallows, warblers, and Baltimore Oriole. As you drive along the gravel entrance road listen for Black-throated Green and Prairie Warblers, plus Ovenbird.

Hirst Wildlife Area

From Riverland Conservation Area, return to U.S. Highway 4, turn right, and proceed for 0.7 mile to a sign indicating a left turn to reach U.S. Highway 3. Turn left and go 0.7 mile to a T at the junction with U.S. Highway 3 (called South Main Street). Turn right to go north on U.S. Highway 3 for 0.5 mile and then turn left onto Queen Street. In 0.7 mile you will come to Hirst Wildlife Area on your left. Pull in and park by the metal gate. *Don't block the gate.* This area provides worthwhile birding from spring through fall. In fall, hunters frequent the area, so you may want to avoid it then.

From the gate there is an old road leading a quarter-mile through the woods to Hirst Marsh. Your first good view of this large open marsh will be on your right. Look for migrant Hooded Mergansers. From spring through fall check for Pied-billed Grebe, American Bittern, Great Blue Heron, Sharp-shinned and Broad-winged Hawks, Spotted Sandpiper, and Louisiana Waterthrush. A Black Tern was seen here in May 1990.

From your first vantage point, continue along the old road. During spring and fall migration this is a rewarding area for passerines such as Eastern Wood-Pewee, Brown Creeper, Winter Wren, Ruby-crowned and Golden-crowned Kinglets, Bicknell's and Hermit Thrushes, Solitary and Red-eyed Vireos, Tennessee, Black-throated Green, Pine, and Black-and-white Warblers, Ovenbird, and Northern Waterthrush. Walking another 0.2 mile along the road, from the first stop, will bring you to the dam at the back side of the marsh. Walk up onto the raised dike beside the dam to obtain a clear view from which to scan the marsh.

Return along the old road back to your car. This stop concludes the Concord-area trip.

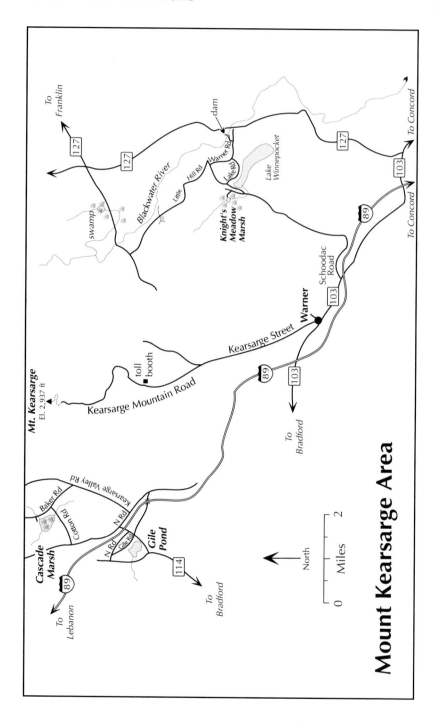

Mount Kearsarge Area

K. MOUNT KEARSARGE AREA

This trip comprises a collection of varied habitats ranging from marsh to mountain. The major feature of this area is the almost-3,000-foot spruce-covered Mount Kearsarge. You will find traveler services at most exits off Interstate 89. *Allow a half-day for this trip,* which is productive during spring, summer, and fall.

Gile Pond

Take Exit 10 off Interstate 89. From the end of the exit ramp go west for 0.3 mile and turn right at the 4-way intersection onto Gile Road (dirt). In 0.3 mile there is a pull-off on the left where you can launch a canoe or other small craft on Gile Pond. This spot will give you a view of the pond. Continue another 0.1 mile along Gile Road to another pull-off on the left. This is a picturesque spot and a nice place for a picnic. The area is encompassed by Shadow Hill State Forest.

Migrants to look for include Ring-necked Duck, Bufflehead, Common Merganser, and Osprey. Summer residents include Wood Duck, Broad-winged Hawk, Spotted Sandpiper, Belted Kingfisher, Northern Flicker, Pileated Woodpecker, Eastern Wood-Pewee, Great Crested Flycatcher, Eastern Kingbird, Tree Swallow, Brown Creeper, Veery, Red-eyed Vireo, and Yellow, Yellow-rumped, Black-throated Blue, Pine, and Black-and-white Warblers. Spring, especially toward dusk, is a likely time to hear the American Bittern's strange *glunk-ga-glunk* call that sounds a little like an old hand-pump.

Cascade Marsh

From Gile Pond, return to the junction with Interstate 89 and proceed under the highway a short distance to the T. Turn right onto North Road heading toward Winslow State Park. In 0.4 mile turn left onto Kearsarge Valley Road, again heading toward Winslow State Park. Follow this road for 1.6 miles, turning left onto Baker Road (dirt). In 1.2 miles, immediately after crossing over Cascade Brook, turn left and follow the brook for 0.1 mile to Cascade Marsh on the left.

There is a sign here indicating that Cascade Marsh is managed by New Hampshire Fish and Game Department as a Waterfowl Management Area. Pull into the small parking area on the left near the sign and the dam. (There is additional parking space on the opposite side of the road.)

Cascade Marsh.

You can launch a canoe, just above the dam, to explore the marsh, or you can obtain an adequate view from the dam with a spotting scope. The marsh has a Beaver lodge, Wood Duck boxes, and an impressive list of bird species that makes this a hotspot, especially during migration. A visit in summer is also worthwhile for nesting ducks, and to enjoy the water-lilies and Pickerelweed in bloom.

Migrants to look for include Northern Pintail, Blue-winged Teal, Ring-necked Duck, Common Merganser, Osprey, Solitary Sandpiper, Palm Warbler, and Pine Siskin. Summer residents include Pied-billed Grebe; American and Least (rare) Bitterns; Hooded Merganser; Northern Harrier; Red-tailed Hawk; American Kestrel; Virginia Rail; Spotted Sandpiper; Belted Kingfisher; Yellow-bellied Sapsucker; Northern Flicker; Alder, Willow, and Great Crested Flycatchers; Eastern Kingbird; Tree, Northern Rough-winged, Bank, and Barn Swallows; Winter, Sedge (rare), and Marsh Wrens; Chestnut-sided, Black-throated Green, Pine, and Canada Warblers; American Redstart; Ovenbird; Scarlet Tanager; Rose-breasted Grosbeak; Rufous-sided Towhee; Swamp and White-throated Sparrows; and Baltimore Oriole.

Return to Baker Road, turn right, go 0.4 mile, and turn right again onto Cotton Road. In a quarter-mile you will come to a small wooden bridge at the back side of Cascade Marsh. There is a pull-off on the left just before the bridge. This spot provides another view of the marsh. From here, return on Baker Road and Kearsarge Valley Road to Interstate 89. Go south on the Interstate.

Mount Kearsarge

Take Exit 9 off Interstate 89. (You will find food and gasoline at this exit.) From Interstate 89 follow State Route 103 east for 1.2 miles and turn left onto Kearsarge Street at the leading edge of the town of Warner. When you turn left onto Kearsarge Street, stay to the left of the monument. As you drive the 5.0 miles from Warner to the toll booth (at the entrance to Rollins State Park), you will climb steadily uphill and have a scenic view on your left. In July 1994 a Rufous Hummingbird spent a few days visiting a feeder at a private residence along this road.

At the entrance to Rollins State Park you must stop and pay a small fee to take the road to the top of 2,937-foot Mount Kearsarge. Although the 3.5-mile road is steep, it is paved and in good condition. Shortly after the entrance, there is a pull-off on the left with picnic tables, water, and a latrine.

Species to look for on Mount Kearsarge include Yellow-bellied Sapsucker, Pileated Woodpecker, Least Flycatcher, Golden-crowned Kinglet, Swainson's, Hermit, and Wood Thrushes, Solitary Vireo, Nashville, Magnolia, Black-throated Blue, Blackburnian, and Canada Warblers, Rose-breasted Grosbeak, Indigo Bunting, Rufous-sided Towhee, White-throated Sparrow, Dark-eyed Junco, and Evening Grosbeak.

Blackburnian Warbler
Georges Dremeaux

Looking southwest from Mount Kearsarge.

From the entrance, proceed 1.6 miles to a pull-off on the left. This stop provides a nice view to the south looking toward Mount Monadnock. Listen for Black-throated Blue, Black-throated Green, and Blackburnian Warblers. Continue another 0.5 mile up the road to the next pull-off on the right, with a clear view to the east. Another 0.1 mile will bring you to the next overlook on the left, with a view to the southwest. This is another worthwhile spot from which to look and listen for chickadees and warblers.

In 0.2 mile after the preceding overlook, stop at the grassy pull-off on the left. A short walk along the edge of the road will bring you to a small swamp. Check for woodpeckers, Winter Wren, and warblers. Another 0.8 mile will bring you to the parking lot at the end of the road, where you will find picnic tables and a latrine.

There is a rough, rocky path leading approximately 0.5 mile from the parking lot to the top of the mountain. If you undertake this hike, stop along the path wherever you hear "chip" notes. Pishing may bring out an assortment of passerines. From the top of the mountain there is a panoramic view in all directions. The bare rock at the summit reveals glacial striations, distinctive scrape-marks left behind by a passing glacier.

Birds to look for at the summit include American Kestrel, Common Raven, Black-capped Chickadee, American Pipit (migrant), Cedar Waxwing, Tennessee, Black-throated Blue, Black-throated Green, and Blackburnian Warblers, and Dark-eyed Junco. During the fall, northerly or easterly winds may bring a large flight of hawks over the mountain.

Return to State Route 103, turn left, and follow the directions in the next section for Knight's Meadow Marsh.

Knight's Meadow Marsh

From the junction of State Route 103 and Kearsarge Street in Warner, go south on State Route 103 for 1.2 miles and turn left onto Schoodac Road, just before the junction with Interstate 89. Follow Schoodac Road for 4.2 miles, turning left onto an unmarked dirt road with a sign that reads "Knight's Meadow Public Access." In 0.4 mile bear left onto a smaller dirt road and proceed for 0.3 mile to the marsh.

The sign by the dam indicates that this is a New Hampshire Fish and Game Department Waterfowl Management Area. There is a parking area, and a spot to launch a canoe or other small boat. A path leads through the trees along the left side of the inlet and will take you 0.2 mile to where you will have a much better view of the marsh.

During spring and fall look for Ring-necked Duck, Lesser Scaup, Common Goldeneye, Bufflehead, Hooded and Common Mergansers, Osprey, and Solitary Sandpiper. In summer you should find Wood Duck, Eastern Phoebe, Tree Swallow, Blue Jay, Black-capped Chickadee, Yellow-rumped Warbler, and Song Sparrow.

Blackwater Reservoir

Return to Schoodac Road, turn left, and go 0.5 mile. Turn right onto Lake Road, go 1.0 mile, turn right onto Warner Road (unmarked), go 0.5 mile, and turn left into the Blackwater Dam parking area. You can walk out onto the top of the dam for a view up the river.

As you leave the parking area, turn right, go north on Warner Road for 1.1 miles, and turn right onto Little Hill Road. In 1.8 miles this becomes a dirt road. Drive slowly with your windows down along this stretch and listen for warblers and other passerines. In another 0.4 mile there is an old road that cuts across Little Hill Road. You can park here and explore both sides. To the right the old road runs alongside the river. To the left it passes by a small pond (on the left); then in another 100 yards it comes to a fork in a wide grassy clearing. Try pishing for warblers and other passerines. Philadelphia Vireo is sometimes recorded here during migration.

Continue along Little Hill Road for another 1.2 miles to where the road ends at a T. Turn right and go 0.4 mile to a narrow bridge crossing the Blackwater River. Park on the left just before or after the bridge and bird from the edge of the road. In another 0.5 mile there is a stream-crossing with a marshy area on the right. Look here for woodpeckers and flycatchers. Continue for 0.3 mile to another stream-crossing with a swamp on the left. Louisiana Waterthrush is sometimes found in this area during May and June. Listen for Barred and Northern Saw-whet Owls calling at night.

Continue for 1.3 miles and turn right onto Route 127. Follow this road for 9.5 miles to Route 103. Turn right and follow Route 103 for 0.8 mile to Interstate 89 (Exit 7), where this trip ends.

Black-throated Green Warbler
Shawneen Finnegan

Peterborough Loop

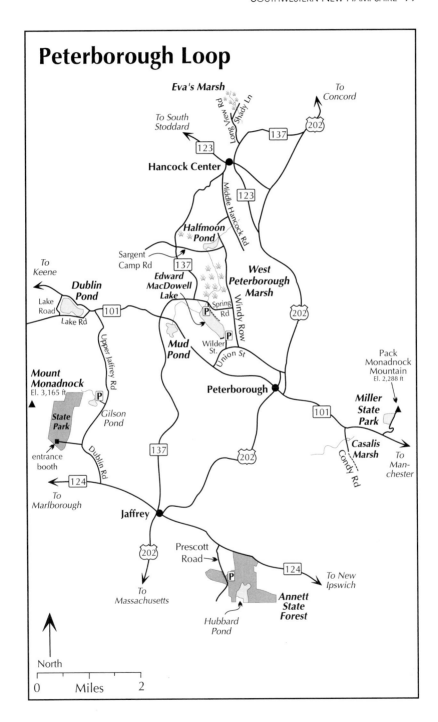

L. PETERBOROUGH LOOP

The starting-point for this loop is the town of Peterborough at the junction of U.S. Highway 202 and State Route 101. Modest accommodations and most traveler services can be found in Peterborough. Thornton Wilder's play *Our Town* was based on this quaint New Hampshire town. Spring, summer, and fall are rewarding times to visit. *Allow at least a half-day for this loop.*

Pack Monadnock Mountain

From the junction of U. S. Highway 202 south and State Route 101 in Peterborough (at the set of lights) go east on State Route 101 for 3.8 miles and follow the signs to Miller State Park (small fee). This is the state's oldest park, established in 1891. You can drive the steep, paved road 1.3 miles to the top of 2,288-foot Pack Monadnock Mountain. This is a reliable location for fall hawk-watching, especially with a northwest wind. The spring hawk migration here is less productive than that in the fall, but can be worth watching if winds are out of the south.

Mid-September is the best time to view kettles of Broad-winged Hawks. They are usually accompanied by a few Ospreys, Bald Eagles, Northern Harriers, Sharp-shinned and Cooper's Hawks, American Kestrels, Merlins, and Common Ravens. There is an organized hawkwatch on the summit.

Looking north from the summit of Pack Monadnock Mountain.

Common Redpoll
Georges Dremeaux

Casalis Marsh

Return to State Route 101, turn right (west), go 1.1 miles, and turn left on Condy Road. Follow this road for 0.1 mile to Casalis Marsh on the left. Look for waterfowl and flycatchers. Here you might pick up Wood Duck, Virginia Rail, Eastern Wood-Pewee, and Common Yellowthroat, among other birds.

Edward MacDowell Lake

From Casalis Marsh, return to State Route 101, turn left, go 4.7 miles, and turn right on Union Street. In 0.5 mile turn left onto Wilder Street, at the sign indicating that this is the way to Edward MacDowell Lake, named for the nineteenth-century composer. As you drive the 0.3 mile up Wilder Street, watch the brushy areas on the edge of the road. They can be productive in spring for such birds as Eastern Phoebe, Hermit Thrush, Northern Cardinal, American Tree and Song Sparrows, Dark-eyed Junco, and even Common Redpoll. At the 0.3-mile mark you will pass through the entrance gate; continue another 0.1 mile to the office. There are restrooms, a public phone, and a few picnic tables here.

This is another United States Army Corps of Engineers flood-control project. The lake was formed by damming Nubanusit Brook. The 1,000-foot dam was completed in 1950 at a cost of $2 million and will impound 4.2 million gallons of water.

From 8 am to 4 pm, during the summer season, you can drive out across the dam to an additional picnic area with cooking grills and restrooms. If the gate is closed, you can walk out onto the dam to view the lake. Look for migrant waterfowl.

Return to Union Street, turn left, go 0.4 mile, and turn left onto Windy Row. Follow this for 1.2 miles and turn left onto Spring Road (unmarked). In 0.1 mile you will see a sign on the left (near a gate) for the Game Preserve. You can walk down the road behind the gate to look for woodland passerines.

Continue along Spring Road for another 0.7 mile and turn left onto Richardson Road. This road leads 0.2 mile to a parking area at another gate. Walk down the road behind the gate for about 100 yards to reach the lake. Walking 400 yards farther will bring you within sight of the dam. There is a clear view of the lake from several vantage points along this road. Scan for waterfowl.

After walking back to your car, return to Spring Road and turn left. In 0.1 mile there is a sign on the right for West Peterborough Marsh. There is a path to the right of the sign which leads one-quarter mile through the woods to the marsh. Listen for wood warblers along the path. Check the marsh for waterfowl and flycatchers.

Halfmoon Pond

Continuing along Spring Road for another 0.3 mile will bring you to the junction with State Route 137. Turn right and follow State Route 137 north for 1.9 miles to a small crossroad. Turn right onto Sargent Camp Road. This, merely a small dirt road, is easy to miss. There is, however, a sign reading "Boston University Sargent Camp." Follow Sargent Camp Road for 0.8 mile to Halfmoon Pond on the left. In another 0.2 mile you will come to another view of Halfmoon Pond at the boat-launch. During spring and fall migration look for waterfowl and Osprey.

Eva's Marsh

Follow Sargent Camp Road for 0.4 mile to where it ends at Windy Row (not marked). Turn left and go 0.7 mile to a marsh on both sides of the road. Look for birds such as Virginia Rail, Northern Flicker, Eastern Phoebe, and Alder and Great Crested Flycatchers.

Continue for another 0.4 mile to a T. Turn left onto Middle Hancock Road (unmarked) and proceed for 1.4 miles to State Route 137. Bear right on State Route 137, go 0.3 mile to Hancock Center, and bear right to stay on State Route 137. In 0.2 mile turn left (still on Route 137), go 0.6 mile, and turn left on Long View Road (leaving Route 137). Immediately after turning onto Long View Road you will see a marshy area on the left. This may be worth a quick stop.

Continue for 0.8 mile and bear right onto Shady Lane (unmarked). Proceed for 0.2 mile on this dirt road to Eva's Marsh on the left. There is a sign indicating that this is a New Hampshire Fish and Game Department Waterfowl Management Area. During spring and fall look for migrating waterfowl such as Hooded and Common Mergansers. During summer look for Wood Duck, Mallard, Eastern Phoebe, and Eastern Kingbird.

Mud Pond, spring waterfowl stop-over.

Mud Pond

From Eva's Marsh, return on Shady Lane and Long View Road to State Route 137. If you need supplies, there is a small grocery store and a gas station in Hancock Center. From Hancock Center, follow State Route 137 south for 3.0 miles to a large marsh on the left. There is room to pull off on the right to check for marsh birds.

Continue south on State Route 137 for 3.8 miles to State Route 101. Turn left onto State Route 101 and go 0.3 mile to a pull-off on the right by a large open marsh. This is Mud Pond. During migration look for Wood Duck, Northern Shoveler, Ring-necked Duck, Common Merganser, and other waterfowl.

Dublin Pond

From Mud Pond turn left to follow State Route 101 west for 3.8 miles; then turn left onto Lake Road. In 0.5 mile there is a small, paved boat-launch on the left with a clear view of Dublin Pond. Look for migrating waterfowl, including scoters, Bufflehead, and mergansers.

From the boat-launch, continue around Dublin Pond for 0.2 mile to the T. Turn left and go 1.1 miles to State Route 101. Along this section you will have several opportunities to view the pond from the road.

Mount Monadnock

When you reach State Route 101, turn right, go 0.1 mile, and turn right onto Upper Jaffrey Road. Proceed for 3.3 miles to Monadnock State Park, Gilson Pond Area, on the right. There are picnic tables by the Birchtoft Trail Head.

Continue for another 1.4 miles to the Monadnock State Park main entrance. Turn right on the access road and go 0.7 mile to the entrance booth (fee). There is a state-run campground, picnic area, restrooms, and hiking trails. In particular, you can climb to the top of Mount Monadnock, which holds the distinction of being the most-climbed mountain in North America. ("Monadnock" is an Algonquin word and a geologic term for an erosional-remnant mountain that stands by itself.) On a clear day the view from the summit will include the Atlantic Ocean and at least one point in each of the five other New England states.

Mount Monadnock is a 3,165-foot spruce-covered mountain that provides fine sub-boreal birding in spring, summer, and fall. Birds to look for include Olive-sided and Yellow-bellied Flycatchers (migrants), Common Raven, Winter Wren, Golden-crowned Kinglet, Gray-cheeked (migrant) and Swainson's Thrushes, Nashville, Magnolia, Yellow-rumped, Blackpoll (migrant), Mourning (migrant), and Canada Warblers, White-throated Sparrow, Dark-eyed Junco, Red and White-winged Crossbills (winter), and Pine Siskin.

Annett State Forest

As you leave Monadnock State Park, turn right on Dublin Road (which was called Upper Jaffrey Road in Dublin), go 1.3 miles, and turn left at the T onto State Route 124. Proceed for 4.3 miles and turn right on Prescott Road. In 1.1 miles turn left into Annett State Park. This is a day-use state park with restrooms and picnic areas. Look for Dark-eyed Junco and Evening Grosbeak.

Return 3 miles to the blinking light in the center of Jaffrey and turn right, following U.S. Highway 202 north for 6 miles to the junction with State Route 101 in Peterborough. This routing closes the loop.

Swainson's Thrush
Georges Dremeaux

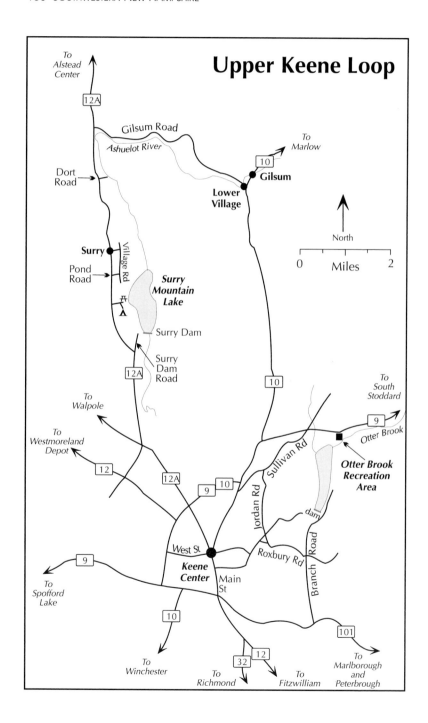

Upper Keene Loop

To Alstead Center

12A

Gilsum Road

Ashuelot River

To Marlow

10

Gilsum

Dort Road

Lower Village

North

0   Miles   2

Surry

Village Rd

Pond Road

Surry Mountain Lake

Surry Dam

Surry Dam Road

12A

To Walpole

To Westmoreland Depot

12

12A

9   10

10

To South Stoddard

9

Otter Brook

Otter Brook Recreation Area

Sullivan Rd

Jordan Rd

dam

Branch Road

West St

Keene Center

Main St

Roxbury Rd

9

To Spofford Lake

10

To Winchester

32   12

To Richmond

To Fitzwilliam

101

To Marlborough and Peterbrough

M. Keene Loop

The starting-point for this loop is the western edge of the city of Keene at the junction of State Routes 101 and 12. All traveler services can be found in the city of Keene. This area provides worthwhile birding during spring and fall migration as well as during the summer nesting season. *Allow a full day for this loop.*

For tourist information on the Keene area contact:

- Keene Chamber of Commerce
  8 Central Square
  Keene, NH 03431
  603/352-1303

Surry Mountain Lake

From the junction of State Route 101 with State Routes 9, 10, and 12, go north on State Route 12 for 2.5 miles and take the exit for State Route 12A. Turn right at the end of the exit ramp onto State Route 12A, and go 0.7 mile to a set of lights. From the lights go straight to continue on State Route 12A toward Surry for 1.7 miles and bear right at the fork onto Surry Dam Road. Follow Surry Dam Road for 0.4 mile to the small parking area on the right.

This is yet another United States Army Corps of Engineers flood-control project. The 1,800-foot dam was completed in 1942 at a cost of $1.75 million and holds 10.6 million gallons of water. The area near the dam is open Monday through Friday from 8 am to 3 pm during the summer. In season, you can drive up the hill past the maintenance buildings and over the dam, to a picnic area.

Birds to look for include Turkey Vulture, Downy Woodpecker, Black-capped Chickadee, Red-breasted and White-breasted Nuthatches, American Robin, Northern Cardinal, and Dark-eyed Junco.

Return to State Route 12A, turn right, and go north for 1.0 mile to the Surry Mountain Recreation Area on your right, open 8 am to 8 pm from Memorial Day through Labor Day. As you turn into the recreation area, the road on the right leads to a private campground; the road straight ahead leads to the picnic area. From the picnic area there is a clear view of the lake.

Continue north on State Route 12A for 0.5 mile and turn right on Pond Road. In 0.1 mile bear right on Village Road and go 0.2 mile to a gate. The road beyond the gate leads to the picnic area. Park on the left near the gate and walk out to the left beyond the gate for a nice view overlooking the lake. Look for Pied-billed Grebe in the marshy area at the north end of the lake. Common Snipes nest here in June. You may see River Otter. A scope is certainly helpful here.

Return to State Route 12A, turn right, and continue north for 1.8 miles. Turn right on Dort Road, and in 0.1 mile you will come to a gate. Walk out the old road beyond the gate. This area can be productive for migrating passerines in spring and fall.

Continuing north on State Route 12A for 1.2 miles, turn right on Gilsum Road. The 4-mile drive across Gilsum Road to State Route 10 is very scenic, with the Ashuelot River staying close to the road on your right. There are many pull-offs that you can use to search for birds in the trees bordering the river.

Otter Brook Lake

When you reach State Route 10, turn right and head south for 5.0 miles to the junction with State Route 9. Turn left on State Route 9 and go 1.7 miles to the Otter Brook Recreation Area (no fee). This stop is included here more for its facilities than for its birds, although you should find Cedar Waxwing, Chestnut-sided and Black-throated Green Warblers, Common Yellowthroat, and Scarlet Tanager.

This is another United States Army Corps of Engineers flood-control project. The lake was formed by damming Otter Brook. The 1,288-foot dam was completed in 1958 at a cost of $4 million and will hold 6 million gallons of water. The park is open daily from 7 am to 3 pm during the summer. Facilities include restrooms, picnic tables, cooking grills, and a beach for swimming.

As you leave the park, turn left on State Route 9 and go 0.7 mile, turning left on Sullivan Road (follow the signs to Otter Brook Dam). Drive 1.3 miles and turn left on Jordan Road. In another 1.3 miles turn left on Roxbury Road, go 0.9 mile, and turn left onto Branch Road (unmarked) at a 4-way intersection. Drive up the hill with Otter Brook on your left. After 0.6 mile bear left at the fork and proceed 0.2 mile to the office and restrooms at the base of the dam. (This area is open during the summer season only.) Return to Branch Road and take a sharp left to continue 0.3 mile to the top of the dam, where there is a parking area on the left. You can walk out on top of the dam to view the lake. Scan for waterfowl.

Chesterfield Gorge and Spofford Lake

Turn around here and go south on Branch Road, past the 4-way intersection where you came out, and in another 2.3 miles you will come to State Route 101. Turn right, proceeding west on State Route 101 for 3.3 miles to the junction with State Route 9. State Route 101 ends here, but continue straight (west) on State Route 9 for another 5.6 miles to Chesterfield Gorge State Wayside Area. This area has picnic tables, restrooms, and a tourist information center with a small museum featuring antique farming tools. A trail will take you on a one-mile hike around the scenic gorge.

From Chesterfield Gorge take State Route 9 west for 2.6 miles, turn right onto State Route 9A, and proceed for 0.1 mile to a parking area and boat-launch on your left. From the boat-launch there is a clear view of Spofford Lake. During migration look for Common Loon, Horned and Red-necked Grebes, Green-winged Teal, Lesser Scaup, Oldsquaw, all three scoters, Bufflehead, and Common Merganser. Tundra Swan has been recorded here in the fall. The shoreline of Spofford Lake is highly developed, so it is difficult to obtain any other unobstructed view of the lake.

The North End of Pisgah State Park

Pisgah State Park is a large (13,000-acre) undeveloped park, and is the state's largest. There are numerous old roads and trails throughout the park which are open to foot traffic but not to motorized vehicles. There are no camping or restroom facilities at this park. Specialties of Pisgah include Yellow-bellied Flycatcher (migrant), Wood Thrush, White-eyed (rare) and Yellow-throated Vireos, Cape May Warbler (migrant), and Purple Finch. After sunset listen for Whip-poor-wills.

From Spofford Lake, return to State Route 9 and continue west for 0.5 mile to the junction with State Route 63. Turn left, go south on State Route 63 for 1.1 miles, and turn left on Old Chesterfield Road (following the sign to Horseshoe Trail Head). In 0.2 mile bear right on Horseshoe Road. Half way along the 1.4 miles to the parking area and trailhead this road changes from paved to gravel. At the parking area you will find a mailbox with a trail guide for Horseshoe Trail, and another mailbox with Pisgah State Park maps.

Near the parking area you should find Blue-winged, Yellow, and Chestnut-sided Warblers, American Redstart, Rose-breasted Grosbeak, Indigo Bunting, and Field Sparrow. Along the trail listen for Eastern

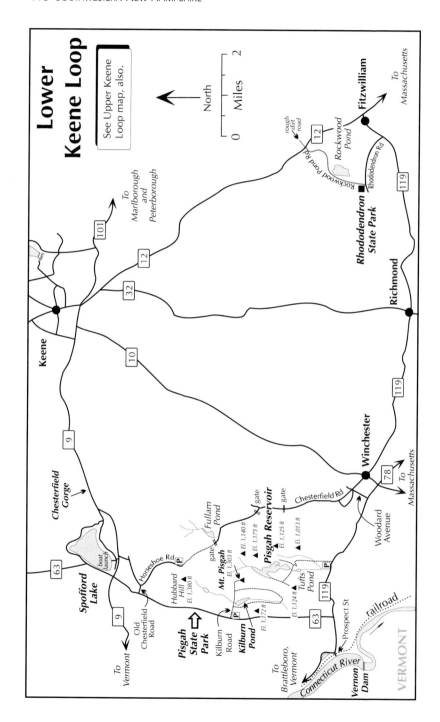

Horseshoe Trail Head at Pisgah State Park.

Wood-Pewee, Yellow-bellied (migrant) and Least Flycatchers, Veery, Wood Thrush, Cedar Waxwing, and Red-eyed Vireo. Stay alert in this area for Ruffed Grouse and Wild Turkey. Be sure to use plenty of insect repellent, or the swarms of mosquitoes will carry you away!

Return to State Route 63 and turn left to continue south. In 3.2 miles turn left into a parking area for the Kilburn Road Trail Head. Park maps are available here, also. This trail leads to Pisgah Mountain Trail, which will take you to 1,303-foot Mount Pisgah.

Connecticut River

Continue south on State Route 63 for 3.7 miles to its junction with State Route 119. Turn right on State Route 119, go 1.3 miles, take a sharp left on Prospect Street, and take a quick right to the boat-launch area. This is an inlet from the Connecticut River. Continue past the boat-launch and turn right on an old railroad bed that parallels the river. Vernon Dam is located just south of here, creating a wide slow-moving section of the river. This part of the Connecticut River can be productive for waterfowl during both spring and fall migrations.

Look for Red-throated Loon, Pied-billed and Horned Grebes, Snow and Canada Geese, American Black Duck, Mallard, Northern Pintail, Gadwall, American Wigeon, Canvasback, Greater Scaup, Common Goldeneye, Hooded and Common Mergansers, Common Moorhen (rare), and American Coot. If you are especially lucky, you may even see an American Golden-Plover in the grassy areas (most likely in fall). There is at least one confirmed record of a Greater White-fronted Goose mixed in with a flock of Canada Geese on the river.

The South End of Pisgah State Park

After 0.7 mile along the railroad bed turn right to return to State Route 119. Go right and follow State Route 119 for 2.1 miles back to the junction with State Route 63. Continue on State Route 119 for another 2.1 miles and turn left into the parking area for Reservoir Trail in Pisgah State Park. The trail starts out climbing a steep hill at the right end of the parking area. Park maps are available at the trailhead.

Resume your route east on State Route 119 for another 2.7 miles (passing by a picturesque covered bridge along the way), then turn left onto Woodard Avenue (following the signs for Pisgah State Park). In 0.6 mile turn left on Chesterfield Road (unmarked) at the 5-way intersection. Follow this road (which changes from paved to gravel) for 5.4 miles to a fork in the road. (At the 2.6-mile mark and the 3.5-mile mark you will pass through metal gates that are open from late spring through summer.)

After you reach the gravel section, drive slowly with your windows down, looking and listening for Broad-winged Hawk, Great Crested Flycatcher, Red-breasted Nuthatch, Brown Creeper, Solitary Vireo, Black-throated Green Warbler, and Northern and Louisiana Water-thrushes.

From the fork (at the 5.4-mile mark), continue straight for another 0.2 mile to a parking area and trailheads. Just before the parking area there is a brushy area on the right. Listen for Golden-winged Warbler singing from the small saplings.

Return 0.2 mile and drive out the other side of the fork for 0.1 mile to a view of Fullam Pond. Canada Geese nest here. You should be able to see the goslings any time from late May through June.

Rhododendron State Park

Return to the fork and drive the 5.4 miles back to Woodard Avenue at the 5-way intersection. Continue straight past Woodard Avenue for another 0.7 mile to State Route 119 at a set of lights. From the lights go straight and follow State Route 119 east for 13.3 miles. Go left on Rhododendron Road, following the sign for Rhododendron State Park. Proceed for 2.0 miles, turn right on Rockwood Pond Road, and follow the signs into Rhododendron State Park. A small fee is charged to enter the park, which provides picnic tables and latrines.

This park preserves the largest stand of native wild Rosebay (or Great Laurel) Rhododendrons (*Rhododendron maximum*) in the state. Described by fans as "a rhododendron jungle," the sight can be very impressive. The best time to visit to see the rhododendrons in bloom is during July. A series of short trails criss-crosses the park, with trail guides available at the trailhead. The trails are clear, well-marked, and easy to follow. Interpretive signs indicate the names of the various species of trees and plants. Some of the more interesting plants found during April and May include Bunchberry, Wild Columbine, Jack-in-the-pulpit, Painted Trillium, Starflower, and Wild-Oats. Plants blooming during June and July include Checkerberry (Wintergreen), Mountain Laurel, Pink Lady's-slipper (Moccasin-flower), and Pink Azalea.

Rhododendron State Park is one of the best places in New Hampshire to find nesting warblers such as Northern Parula, Chestnut-sided, Black-throated Blue, Yellow-rumped, Black-throated Green, Cerulean (rare), Black-and-white, and Canada Warblers, and Common Yellowthroat. Other nesting species to expect include Eastern Wood-Pewee, Brown Creeper, Veery, Hermit and Wood Thrushes, and Scarlet Tanager. You may also find Ruby-throated Hummingbirds at the wildflowers and rhododendrons. June or early July is the time to visit to find nesting birds.

Return to State Route 119, turn left, and go 0.9 mile to the junction with State Route 12. Turn left and follow State Route 12 north for 12 miles to the junction with State Route 101 in Keene to conclude this loop.

Oldsquaws
Shawneen E. Finnegan

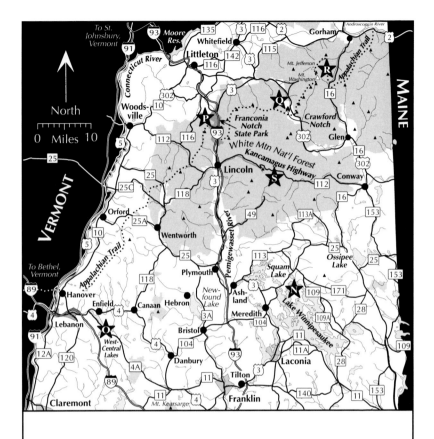

CENTRAL NEW HAMPSHIRE

 Lake Winnipesaukee Loop

 West-Central Lakes

 Franconia Notch Loop

 Crawford and Jefferson Notches

 Mount Washington Valley

 Kancamagus Highway

Chapter 3:

CENTRAL NEW HAMPSHIRE

This section spans the state from Vermont in the west to Maine in the east, and runs from the Tilton/Franklin area north through the White Mountains. The main features of central New Hampshire are the famous vacation areas of Lake Winnipesaukee and the White Mountains. This is a popular destination for summer vacations, fall foliage-watching, and winter skiing. There are numerous tourist attractions, including The Flume, the Old Man of the Mountain, Mount Washington and the rest of the Presidential Range, the Kancamagus Highway, and Lost River.

Aside from the tourist attractions, there are also several fine birding locations in this region. Much of the mountainous area resides within the White Mountain National Forest, providing plenty of land open to public recreation.

For National Forest information contact:

- Forest Supervisor
  P.O. Box 638
  Laconia, NH 03247
  603/528-8721

If you enjoy hiking, there are miles of trails maintained by the Appalachian Mountain Club (AMC). The main access to this part of the state from southern New Hampshire is via Interstate 93.

Altitude plays a key role in what habitat and bird species you will find in the mountains. Climbing a few hundred feet up a mountain can have the same effect on habitat as driving a hundred miles north would. You will encounter a few different Life Zones in the White Mountains. The Transition Zone is found in the valleys and lower mountain slopes from 1,000 to 1,500 feet above sea level. The Canadian Zone reaches from 1,500 feet up to timberline at about 4,800 feet. The Alpine Zone takes over above timberline, introducing an Alpine Tundra habitat.

You will recognize the Transition Zone by the mixture of Northern Hardwoods and spruce/fir trees of the boreal forest. Birds of this zone include White-breasted Nuthatch, Veery, Yellow-throated and Red-eyed Vireos, Pine and Black-and-white Warblers, Ovenbird, Scarlet Tanager, and Rose-breasted Grosbeak.

Typical birds of the Canadian Zone (boreal forest) include Spruce Grouse, Yellow-bellied Sapsucker, Black-backed Woodpecker, Olive-sided and Yellow-bellied Flycatchers, Gray Jay, Boreal Chickadee, Winter Wren, Golden-crowned Kinglet, Bicknell's and Swainson's Thrushes, Magnolia, Black-throated Blue, Black-throated Green, Blackburnian, Bay-breasted, Blackpoll, and Canada Warblers, Northern Waterthrush, Pine Grosbeak, Red and White-winged Crossbills, and Pine Siskin.

Above timberline in the Alpine Zone there are few nesting birds in New Hampshire. Yet there are some, including American Pipit, White-throated Sparrow, and Dark-eyed Junco.

Magnolia Warbler
Barry W. Van Dusen

White-winged Crossbills
Barry W. Van Dusen

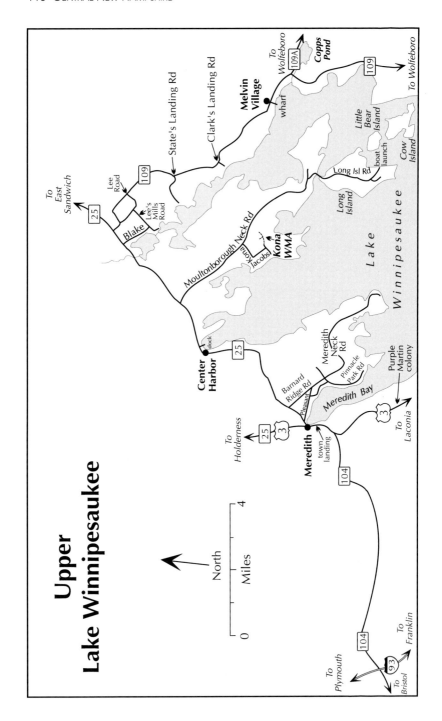

N. LAKE WINNIPESAUKEE AREA

Lake Winnipesaukee, the largest lake in New Hampshire, is a popular summer vacation destination. The name "Winnipesaukee" has been translated as "smile of the Great Spirit," and with 28 miles of length, close to 300 miles of shoreline, and almost 300 islands, the lake can leave a profound smile on the face of the lowliest of travelers. (Not surprisingly, the word "Winnipesaukee" has also been recorded with over 132 different spellings!)

The most highly developed part of the lakeshore is the southwest section near the city of Laconia. However, the other sides of the lake are not nearly as developed and therefore still offer good birding opportunities. The lake is nestled in a picturesque setting with surrounding mountains. Despite a fair amount of boat traffic, Common Loons still nest on the lake.

Spring and fall are the best seasons for this trip, although if you are in the area anyway, summer—or even winter—can be rewarding. Migrants to look for include Horned Grebe, Ring-necked Duck, Common Goldeneye, Bufflehead, and Common Merganser. In winter there is usually open water near boat docks and river inlets, where you may find Ring-necked Duck and Common and Barrow's (rare) Goldeneyes.

All traveler services are available in the Lake Winnipesaukee area, including campgrounds, motels, restaurants, and gas stations. *Allow a full day for this trip.*

For tourist information on the New Hampshire Lakes region contact:

- Lakes Region Association
  P.O. Box 300
  Wolfeboro, NH 03894
  603/569-1117

Meredith Town Landing

This loop begins at the junction of Interstate 93 and State Route 104 just west of Meredith. Take Exit 23 from Interstate 93 and follow State Route 104 east for 8.1 miles to the junction with U.S. Highway 3 in Meredith. If you are interested in seeing a Purple Martin colony, turn right to go south on U.S. Highway 3 for 2.6 miles. Here you can check the active martin houses at the miniature golf course on the left.

Return to the junction with State Route 104, follow U.S. Highway 3 north for 0.7 mile, and turn right into the Meredith Town Landing. This will give you a good location from which to scope Meredith Bay. There is also a boat-launch here (fee for non-residents). Continue north on U.S. Highway 3 for 0.1 mile to the intersection with State Route 25. Turn right to follow State Route 25 east, and go 0.1 mile to a small park on the right with a few picnic tables where you can again scope Meredith Bay.

Meredith Neck

Continue along State Route 25 for 0.1 mile, turn right on Pleasant Street (heading toward Meredith Neck Road), go 0.8 mile, and turn right on Wagon Wheel Trail. Proceed for 0.7 mile, turn right again on Pinnacle Park Road (unmarked), and go 0.1 mile to the boat-launch on the right. There is a chain-link fence here with a gate. This spot gives you a vantage point farther down Meredith Bay, closer to the main part of the lake.

Turn around at the boat-launch, go back on Pinnacle Park Road (past Wagon Wheel Trail, where you just came out), and proceed 0.4 mile to the 4-way intersection. Turn right to follow Meredith Neck Road (unmarked) for 3.8 miles to a boat-launch on the left. There is a large gravel parking area on the right, and a small concrete building on the left next to the town dock. Scope the lake for waterfowl.

Mount Washington Dock

Return on Meredith Neck Road (past the 4-way junction with Pinnacle Park Road), going a total of 4.3 miles from the boat-launch to a fork in the road. Bear right at the fork onto Barnard Ridge Road and continue another 0.9 mile to the junction with State Route 25. Turn right to resume heading east on State Route 25. Go 3.7 miles and turn right onto Lake Street. At the end of this short street you will find a boat-launch, public beach, restrooms (open in summer), and a small parking area that allows no-fee 30-minute parking.

This is also the location of the Center Harbor dock for the *Mount Washington* cruise ship that tours Lake Winnipesaukee. Taking a scenic tour on the *Mount Washington* is a relaxing way to see more of the lake. For information call 603/366-2628.

Kona Wildlife Management Area

Resume your course east on State Route 25 for 1.7 miles and turn right onto Moultonborough Neck Road. Go 2.5 miles, turning right on Kona Road, and go 0.5 mile, turning left on Jacobs Road. In 0.5 mile, at the sign for Stage Road, turn left and in 0.1 mile you will come to a New Hampshire Fish and Game Department sign for Kona Wildlife Management Area. There are several miles of old roads that provide easy foot access to this area.

This is a serene spot to take a bird walk, expecting most of the typical woodland species. Birds to look for are Sharp-shinned Hawk, Northern Goshawk, Ruffed Grouse, Northern Flicker, Pileated Woodpecker, Common Raven, Tufted Titmouse, Red-breasted and White-breasted Nuthatches, Ruby-crowned Kinglet (migrant), Hermit and Wood Thrushes, Solitary and Red-eyed Vireos, Pine Warbler, and Scarlet Tanager.

Long Island

Return to Moultonborough Neck Road, turn right, and go 3.1 miles, bearing right at the fork onto Long Island Road. Proceed for 0.5 mile, crossing over the bridge onto Long Island. Continue out Long Island Road for 1.7 miles, stay left at the fork, and go another 0.3 mile to the boat-launch. Here you can stop to scan the lake for waterfowl. You can see Little Bear Island to your left and Cow Island farther out and to the right. A small herd of Whitetail Deer inhabits the section of woods between the bridge and the boat-launch and can usually be seen along the edge of the road.

State's Landing and Clark's Landing

Retrace your route off the island. At Moultonborough Neck Road bear left and return 5.7 miles to State Route 25. Turn right and go 2.6 miles, turning right onto Blake Road. Go 0.7 mile (becomes gravel) and turn right into the boat-launch area to scan the lake. Continue beyond the boat-launch for 0.2 mile to the T, turn left onto Lee's Mills Road (unmarked), go 0.7 mile to the T, turn right onto Lee Road, and go 0.7 mile to the T and turn right on State Route 109. Follow State Route 109 for 1.1 miles and bear right at the fork to stay on State Route 109. Proceed for 0.7 mile, turn right onto State's Landing Road, and go 1.0 mile to the boat-launch at State's Landing. Here is another scanning opportunity.

Return to State Route 109, turn right, go 1.5 miles, and turn right on Clark's Landing Road. In 0.2 mile you will come to a crossroad. Continue straight down the hill to Clark's Landing boat-launch. Scan for waterfowl.

Return to State Route 109, turn right, go 2.4 miles to Melvin Village, turn right onto Melvin Wharf Road, and proceed to the town wharf. This spot on the lake provides another scoping opportunity.

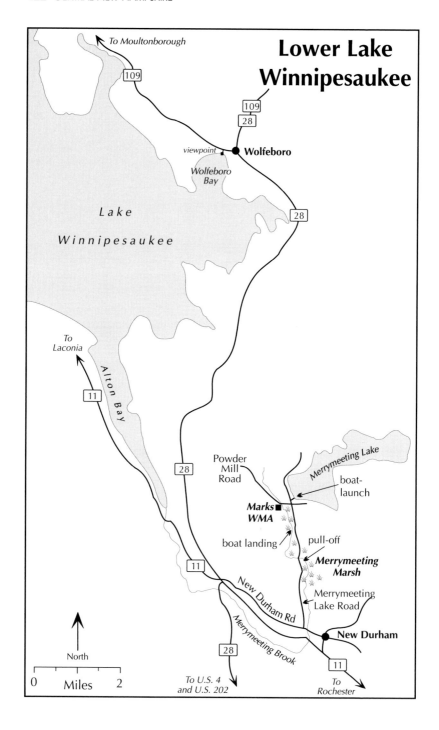

To Moultonborough

109

Lower Lake Winnipesaukee

109
28

viewpoint ● **Wolfeboro**

Wolfeboro Bay

Lake

Winnipesaukee

28

To Laconia

A l t o n   B a y

11

28

Powder Mill Road

Merrymeeting Lake

boat-launch

Marks ■ WMA

boat landing

pull-off

Merrymeeting Marsh

Merrymeeting Lake Road

11

New Durham Rd

● **New Durham**

11

North

0   Miles   2

Merrymeeting Brook

28

To U.S. 4 and U.S. 202

To Rochester

Copps Pond

Return to State Route 109, turn right, go 1.3 miles, and at the sharp bend in the road turn left onto State Route 109A. Go 0.2 mile, turn right onto an unmarked gravel road, and proceed 0.1 mile to the New Hampshire Fish and Game sign for Copps Pond Marsh Waterfowl Management Area. Look for Pied-billed Grebe, American Bittern, Great Blue Heron, Wood Duck, and Spotted Sandpiper.

Wolfeboro Bay

Return to State Route 109, turn left, and go 8.7 miles, entering the town of Wolfeboro. Wolfeboro has been called the quintessential New England town, with white-steepled churches, fine old homes, and splendid scenery. Turn right here, at the one-way sign, into the Wolfeboro Boat Dock (immediately before a large yellow building). There is a boat-launch and parking area with a clear view of Wolfeboro Bay. Scan here for waterfowl. Be aware, however, that this location will be crowded on summer weekends. Food and gasoline are available in town.

Merrymeeting Marsh

Continue south on State Route 109 for 0.2 mile to the junction with State Route 28. Follow State Route 28 south for 11 miles to the rotary. Go three-fourths of the way around the rotary (0.2 mile) and turn right onto New Durham Road. Drive 2.2 miles, turn left on Merrymeeting Lake Road, and go 1.5 miles to Merrymeeting Marsh. Pull off on the right just after the small bridge. Check for American Bittern, Virginia Rail, and Alder, Willow, and Least Flycatchers.

Continue 0.7 mile to Merrymeeting Marsh Boat Landing on the left. There is a gravel parking lot and a boat-launch. This is a convenient spot from which to launch a canoe and head downstream on Merrymeeting Brook. You will be able to pass under the road and into the marshy area that you viewed from the last pull-off.

Birds to look for in the marsh include Great Blue Heron, Wood Duck, Blue-winged Teal (migrant), Bufflehead (migrant), Hooded and Common (migrant) Mergansers, Eastern Kingbird, Tree, Northern Rough-winged, and Barn Swallows, and Marsh Wren. The surrounding woods should have Yellow-rumped and Black-and-white Warblers, Scarlet Tanager, and Chipping and Song Sparrows. Be sure to listen for the hoarse song

Northern Goshawk
Shawneen E. Finnegan

of the Yellow-throated Vireo and the long "warbling" phrases of the appropriately named Warbling Vireo.

From the boat-launch, continue for 0.6 mile to just beyond an askew 4-way intersection and turn right to the boat-launch on Merrymeeting Lake. This is a public access point where you can scan the lake for waterfowl.

Return to the 4-way intersection and turn right onto Powder Mill Road. Drive 0.2 mile to the sign on the left for Marks Tract, Merrymeeting Wildlife Management Area. This is a 286-acre New Hampshire Fish and Game property. Continue a few hundred feet down the road past the sign to a pair of old roads on the left that you can walk along. This is a productive area for wood warblers such as Black-throated Blue, Black-throated Green, and Black-and-white Warblers, American Redstart, and Ovenbird. You may also find Pileated Woodpecker, vireos, Scarlet Tanager, and White-throated Sparrow.

Return to the rotary to conclude this trip. You can follow State Route 28 south to U.S. Highway 4 west to Concord, or take State Route 11 northwest to Laconia. If you have extra time while in the Lake Winnipesaukee area, a worthwhile side-trip is a visit to Annalee's Doll Museum in Meredith, at Reservoir Road and Hemlock Drive (near the start of this trip). This museum contains fascinating doll collections. (Annalee Thorndike, turned down for a business bank loan in the 1950s, began making dolls at her own kitchen table. She later became the area's largest employer.

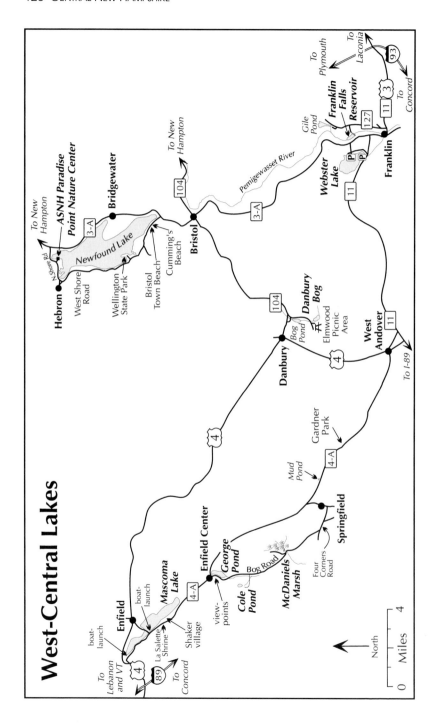

West-Central Lakes

North

Miles

0   4

O. WEST-CENTRAL LAKES

The best seasons for this *all-day trip* are spring, summer, and fall. To reach this group of lakes and marshes in the western portion of the central New Hampshire region, take Interstate 93 to Exit 20, for Tilton and Laconia. Exit the highway onto State Route 11 and U.S. Highway 3. You will find all traveler services at this junction: food, gasoline, lodging, and nearby camping.

Franklin Falls Reservoir

Take State Route 11 west for 4.5 miles (passing through Tilton, Franklin Falls, and Franklin), then turn right to go north on State Route 127 (also called West Bow Street). In 0.2 mile keep left to go straight up the hill on State Route 127. Drive a total of 2.1 miles on State Route 127 to the Franklin Falls Dam on your left. The gate is open in summer from 7 am to 3:30 pm. During the off-season you can park by the gate and walk in. As you proceed along the road from the entrance, you will see a pine grove on the right where you may be able to find Northern Saw-whet Owls roosting. These owls will roost in evergreens or thick shrubbery, often close to eye-level. You are more likely to find them here in winter or early spring than at other times of year. Also look for Eastern Phoebe, Blue Jay, Black-capped Chickadee, Yellow-rumped and Palm (migrant) Warblers, Chipping Sparrow, and Dark-eyed Junco.

Continue north on State Route 127 for another 0.7 mile, turn left on Gile Pond Road, and proceed for 0.2 mile to a boat-launch. You can view the water from here or launch a boat.

Webster Lake

Return to State Route 11, turn right, go west for 0.4 mile, and turn right again to stay on Route 11. In 1.0 mile turn left with State Route 11 and drive another 1.0 mile to Webster Lake on your right. There is a parking area near the beach and a boat-launch where you have a clear view of the lake. During migration look for Common Loon, Horned and Red-necked Grebes, American Black Duck, Gadwall (rare), American Wigeon, all three scoter species, all three merganser species, and Bonaparte's and Ring-billed Gulls. During spring migration Snow Geese often pause here.

Turn around and go 0.1 mile back on State Route 11, turning left on Webster Avenue. Follow Webster Avenue for 0.9 mile to a T. Turn left and pull into the parking area near the beach. There is another clear view of Webster Lake from here. A scope is useful for scanning the lake.

Newfound Lake

As you leave this stop, go straight up the hill, past Webster Avenue, and go 0.5 mile to State Route 3A. Turn left and follow Route 3A for 10.7 miles to Bristol. Turn left in the center of Bristol with State Route 104, go 0.1 mile, and bear right at the fork to stay on State Route 3A north. Follow Route 3A for another 2.1 miles and turn left at the blinking yellow light on West Shore Road. In 0.7 mile pull into the small paved parking lot at Cummings Beach. This will give you a vantage point from which to scope the lake. In another 0.1 mile there is another parking area at Bristol Town Beach. Look for migrant Common Loon, Canada Goose, Common Goldeneye, and Common Merganser.

Drive another 0.9 mile and bear right to stay on West Shore Road. In 1.0 mile turn right into Wellington State Park. The park is open from 9 am to 6:30 pm during the summer and has picnic tables, a beach for swimming, and restrooms. Sparrows and other passerines are often found in the bushes around the edge of the parking lot. You can take a short walk out to the beach to view the lake.

Opposite the park entrance there is a trailhead sign for several trails, including Little Sugarloaf, Big Sugarloaf, Bear Mountain, and Mount Cardigan. These trails range from 0.5 mile to 13 miles in length. Look for Broad-winged Hawk, Northern Flicker, Red-breasted and White-breasted Nuthatches, Yellow-rumped Warbler, White-throated Sparrow, and Dark-eyed Junco.

Continue on West Shore Road for another 4.3 miles and turn right onto North Shore Road (unmarked) by the Hebron Village Store. In 1.3 miles turn right into the paved driveway at New Hampshire Audubon's Paradise Point Nature Center. From the parking lot follow the trail to the nature center, which is open from Memorial Day to Labor Day. The trails are open year round from dawn to dusk. Take the trail directly behind the nature center to reach the lake and scan for waterfowl. There are also woodland trails leading from the nature center where you should find wood warblers. On summer evenings listen for Whip-poor-wills.

Danbury Bog with Ragged Mountain in the background.

Danbury Bog

Resume your course along North Shore Road for 1.0 mile to the junction with State Route 3A. Turn right and follow Route 3A south for 8.6 miles back to the center of Bristol. Make a sharp right around the gas station to follow State Route 104 west for 8 miles to Elmwood. Turn left on the unmarked dirt road (one-way), go 0.3 mile, and pull off on the right by the dam. You can launch a canoe from this spot or just scan Bog Pond.

Immediately after the dam, the dirt road ends at a T. Turn right, heading toward Ragged Mountain, and go 1.0 mile to where the road crosses over Danbury Bog. Just after the bridge, turn left into the Elmwood Picnic Area. From the picnic area you will have a view of the bog. Looking across the bog you can see Ragged Mountain ski area.

Migrants to look for at Danbury Bog include Pied-billed Grebe, Northern Pintail, and Common Merganser. During summer look for American Bittern, Wood Duck, American Black Duck, Mallard, Hooded Merganser, Northern Harrier, Broad-winged Hawk, Killdeer, Belted Kingfisher, Northern Flicker, Olive-sided Flycatcher, Eastern Phoebe, Tree and Barn Swallows, Hermit Thrush, Warbling Vireo, Yellow-rumped Warbler, Red-winged Blackbird, and Baltimore Oriole. Listen for Common Snipe winnowing in spring and summer. In summer the bog blooms with Yellow Pond-lily and Pickerelweed.

Gile State Forest

Return to the dam and continue straight past the one-way dirt road, where you came out, for 0.3 mile to State Route 104. Turn left and go 1.3 miles to the junction with U.S. Highway 4. There is a gas station and grocery store at this intersection. Turn left to take U.S. Highway 4 east (actually going south on this section) for 6.9 miles. Turn left onto the access ramp to State Route 11 west. In 0.75 mile turn right on State Route 4A north. Proceed for 6.9 miles to the boundary of 6,500-acre Gile State Forest. Turn right into Gardner Memorial Wayside Park, where there are picnic tables near the stream. Check around the stream for vireos and warblers.

Continue north on State Route 4A for 1.9 miles to Mud Pond on the right. The marshy stretch between Gardner Park and Mud Pond offers productive birding. Look for Great Blue Heron, Wood Duck, Mallard, Belted Kingfisher, Northern Flicker, Winter Wren, Veery, Yellow-rumped Warbler, Common Yellowthroat, Rose-breasted Grosbeak, White-throated Sparrow, and Red-winged Blackbird. Watch for Moose along this stretch of road.

Olive-sided Flycatcher
Barry W. Van Dusen

McDaniels Marsh

After another 1.3 miles on State Route 4A, turn left onto 4 Corners Road toward Springfield. In 1.0 mile turn right to stay on 4 Corners Road. Continue for 0.8 mile to the stop sign and bear right. Go 0.4 mile and turn right onto Bog Road (unmarked). Proceed for 2.1 miles to McDaniels Marsh on the right. There is a gravel boat-launch and a large open pond. The best birds can be found by canoeing to the marshy area at the far end of the pond. Otherwise, scope from the boat-launch. Look for nesting Pied-billed Grebe, Great Blue Heron, Belted Kingfisher, Yellow-rumped Warbler, and Song Sparrow. During migration you may expect a variety of waterfowl and Osprey.

Enfield Wildlife Management Area

As you leave McDaniels Marsh, turn right, and then immediately bear left at the fork to continue on Bog Road. Go 2.3 miles to a sign on the left for Enfield Wildlife Management Area. Park on the edge of the road near the sign. There is a small bridge leading over the stream with a path continuing for 1.0 mile to Cole Pond. Summer should produce nesting wood warblers along the path. During spring and fall look for migrant waterfowl on the pond.

Continuing on Bog Road for 1.5 miles, you can begin to see George Pond on the right. In another 0.3 mile turn right on a dirt road to an unimproved boat-launch access. Birds to look for in this area include American Black Duck, Downy Woodpecker, Northern Flicker, Willow Flycatcher, Eastern Kingbird, Tree and Barn Swallows, Winter Wren, Veery, Wood Thrush, Yellow, Chestnut-sided, Yellow-rumped, and Black-and-white Warblers, White-throated Sparrow, Red-winged Blackbird, and Common Grackle. Listen for American Bittern and American Woodcock calling at dusk.

Another 0.2 mile on Bog Road will bring you to State Route 4A. At this junction you can pull off on the right to view George Pond. Turn left on State Route 4A and go 3.7 miles if you would like to visit the La Salette Shrine and a Shaker village.

The Shakers established this village in 1793. Today there is a museum which preserves Shaker artifacts and their way of life. You may also visit the gardens and a Shaker store. The Shrine of Our Lady of La Salette is a replica of the famous Marian Shrine in the French Alps.

Mascoma Lake

In 0.7 mile from the La Salette Shrine turn right into the boat-launch parking area. There is a beach for swimming on the opposite side of the road. From the boat-launch you will be in a good position to scope the lake for waterfowl. During fall migration almost anything is possible. In particular, look for Red-throated and Common Loons, Horned Grebe, Snow Goose, Hooded, Common, and Red-breasted Mergansers, and Ruddy Duck.

Going north on State Route 4A for 1.8 miles from the boat-launch, you will come to a dam and another boat-launch on the right providing a view of the lake. Stop and scan for waterfowl.

Go 0.4 mile farther on State Route 4A, left on Route 4, and go 1.6 miles to the junction with Interstate 89. That concludes this loop.

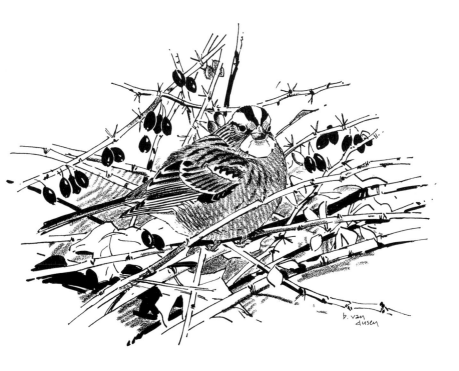

White-throated Sparrow
Barry W. Van Dusen

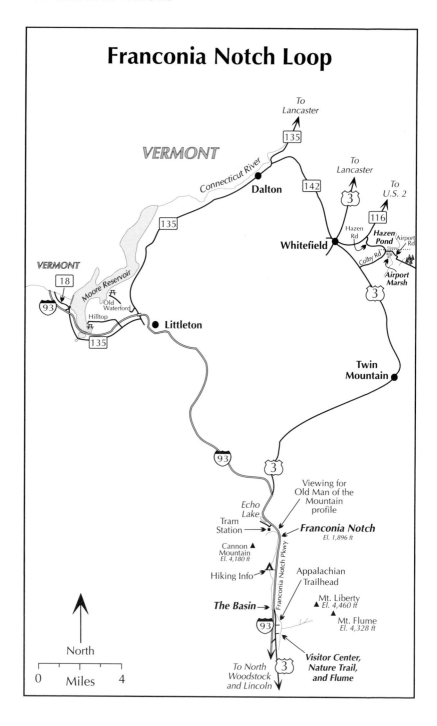

Franconia Notch Loop

To
Lancaster

135

VERMONT

Connecticut River

Dalton

135

18

VERMONT

93

Hilltop

Old
Waterford

Moore Reservoir

142

3

To
Lancaster

116

To
U.S. 2

Hazen
Rd

**Hazen
Pond**

Airport
Rd

Whitefield

Colby Rd

**Airport
Marsh**

3

135

● **Littleton**

**Twin
Mountain** ●

93

3

Viewing for
Old Man of the
Mountain
profile

*Echo
Lake*

Tram
Station →

Franconia Notch
El. 1,896 ft

Cannon ▲
Mountain
El. 4,180 ft

Franconia Notch Pkwy

Hiking Info →

Appalachian
Trailhead

The Basin →

▲ Mt. Liberty
El. 4,460 ft

▲
Mt. Flume
El. 4,328 ft

93

**Visitor Center,
Nature Trail,
and Flume**

↑
North

0   Miles   4

3

*To North
Woodstock
and Lincoln*

P. FRANCONIA NOTCH LOOP

This loop takes you on a tour through scenic Franconia Notch State Park, then to Moore Reservoir in Littleton, and lastly to Whitefield. Franconia and Whitefield provide good birding in spring, summer, and fall. Moore Reservoir is best for spring and fall waterfowl migration. *Allow a full day for this loop.*

Food, lodging, and gasoline are available a few miles south of Franconia Notch in the towns of Lincoln and North Woodstock, as well as just north of the Notch in Bethlehem and Twin Mountain. There is a state-run campground in Franconia Notch State Park.

Franconia Notch State Park

Our tour through Franconia Notch will proceed from south to north. Interstate 93 passes through the notch (a glaciated mountain pass) on the Franconia Notch Parkway at a maximal elevation of 1,896 feet. The Pemigewasset River runs alongside the road through most of the Notch. A visit to Franconia Notch is as much for the natural granite formations and scenic beauty as it is for birds. Take Parkway Exit 1 for The Flume and Park Information Center. The visitor center is open from 9 am to 5 pm spring through fall. A stop here will help to acquaint you with the area.

From the parking lot, as you face the visitor center and look beyond it, you can see Mount Liberty on the left and Mount Flume on the right. Tickets to The Flume may be purchased at the information center, which also houses a cafeteria, restrooms, and a gift shop. The Flume is a natural gorge with sheer walls of granite reaching to a height of 90 feet, a narrow width of 12 feet, and featuring a 45-foot waterfall.

Near the visitor center you will also find picnic tables and the Roaring River Memorial Nature Trail, a 0.3-mile self-guiding walk. Common birds to expect here include Northern Flicker, Golden-crowned Kinglet, Red-eyed Vireo, and Black-throated Blue and Black-throated Green Warblers. From the parking lot you may also see Chimney Swifts and Cedar Waxwings.

As you leave the Flume area, continue north for 0.2 mile to the Appalachian Trail Head access. From this point you can hike the Pemi Trail, paralleling the Pemigewasset River, which leads to several other trails, including the Appalachian Trail.

Continue north for 1.3 miles to the Basin. From the parking area, walk to the left along the paved bicycle path through the underpass to view the Basin, a granite pothole at the base of a waterfall.

Another 1.5 miles will bring you to the Hiker Information Center. From the parking lot, walk through the underpass to the cabin on the west side of the road.   You will find exhibits, trail information, weather advisories, and drinking water. To reach the Lafayette Campground, which is on the west side of the divided highway, continue north to the tramway exit, where you can reverse direction.

Gray Jay
Georges Dremeaux

View from the top of Cannon Mountain, with Barbara Delorey

From the Hiker Information Center, drive 1.6 miles to the Old Man Viewing Area. If you look back across the Parkway, you will have an excellent view of the famous "Old Man of the Mountain", a granite outcropping resembling a human face. Don't expect an enormous image; the face is about 40 feet high, but it is set on a cliff far above the valley floor.

Another 0.3 mile along the Parkway will bring you to the exit for the Cannon Mountain Tramway and Echo Lake Boat Launch. Check around the boat-launch for Alder Flycatcher, Red-breasted Nuthatch, Solitary Vireo, and Yellow-rumped Warbler. Follow the signs to the tramway to reach the ticket station, visitor information center, and cafeteria. The five-minute scenic tram ride is the easy way to reach the 4,180-foot summit of Cannon Mountain. Hiking trails also make the ascent up the mountain.

From the top of the mountain take the 0.3-mile Rim Trail loop. In summer listen for Bicknell's Thrush, which is best found above 3,000 feet and is more often heard than seen. Its song is similar to that of a Veery, but with an inflection at the end. (For additional hints on finding and identifying Bicknell's Thrush in New Hampshire, see Chapter 5.) Along the Rim Trail you should also find Boreal Chickadee, Golden-crowned Kinglet, White-throated Sparrow, and Dark-eyed Junco. Here you can also pick up Gray Jay. Though reclusive during their breeding season—beginning in February and March when the snow is still on the ground—by mid-spring the Gray Jays will appear to be very gregarious. They will travel in small groups, and often appear inquisitive, earning their folk name, "camp robber." Migrants to look for include Ruby-crowned Kinglet and Tennessee, Nashville, Yellow-rumped, Black-throated Green, and Blackpoll Warblers. Peregrine Falcons have nested on the sheer cliffs of the mountain in recent years. In 1981 a pair of Peregrine Falcons nested at Franconia Notch, becoming the first ones in almost three decades to raise young successfully on a natural cliff-site anywhere in the eastern United States.

You may also see a Snowshoe Hare, so-called because of its huge feet, designed for hopping on deep snow. It is also known as Varying Hare because its pelage adapts from summer brown to winter white.

Moore Reservoir

From the Cannon Mountain Tramway take Interstate 93 north 19.7 miles to Exit 44 for State Routes 18 and 135. Go straight across State Route 135, at the end of the exit ramp, to the New England Power Company's Moore Station Visitor Center. There are picnic tables under a grove of trees by the edge of the water. The reservoir was formed by damming the Connecticut River for a hydro-electric station. The station conducts tours from 9 am to 5 pm. You will also find restrooms at the visitor center.

Birding is best during spring and fall waterfowl migration. Look for Red-necked Grebe, Brant (uncommon inland), Red-breasted Merganser, and White-winged and Black Scoters. You should also find Northern Mockingbird and White-crowned Sparrow (spring migrant).

As you leave the visitor station, turn left on State Route 135 and go 1.5 miles to a pull-off on the left for a view of a small inlet from the reservoir. Continue on State Route 135 for 2.4 miles, and turn left on Hilltop Road by the sign indicating New England Power Picnic Area. In 1.8 miles turn left and go 0.1 mile to the picnic and launch area. You will also find cooking grills and a latrine. There is a good overview of the reservoir from which to scope for waterfowl.

Return to State Route 135, turn left, and in 0.9 mile turn left at the T to stay on Route 135 north. In 0.3 mile turn left onto Old Waterford Road, where a sign indicates New England Power Picnic and Boat Launch Area. In 1.8 miles you will come to a cul-de-sac and the picnic and launch area. This spot provides another location to scan for waterfowl.

Whitefield Airport

From the previous stop at Moore Reservoir, follow State Route 135 north for 10.7 miles and turn right on State Route 142 south. Drive 6.0 miles to Whitefield center. (Food and gasoline are available in White-field.) At the stop-sign turn left, go 0.1 mile to a blinking red light, and proceed straight across onto State Route 116 north. Go 1.6 miles and turn right on Hazen Road at the sign for the airport. In 1.3 miles bear left on Airport Road, and in another 0.2 mile pull off on the right at the New Hampshire Fish and Game Department Airport Marsh.

Birds to look for in and around the marsh include Wood Duck, Hooded Merganser, Northern Flicker, Alder, Willow, and Least Fly-catchers, Tree and Bank Swallows, Cedar Waxwing, Warbling and Red-eyed Vireos, Yellow and Chestnut-sided Warblers, American Red-start, Common Yellowthroat, and Song Sparrow. Note that this site is near the northernmost limit of Willow Flycatcher's range in New Hamp-shire.

Walk across the road and up the bank onto the railroad tracks. Turn left and walk along the tracks a short way for a view of Hazen Pond. Birds to look for during nesting season include Virginia Rail, American Wood-cock, Hairy Woodpecker, House Wren, Rusty Blackbird, and Pine Siskin.

Return to your car and continue along Airport Road. As you drive past the grassland on your left, look and listen for Killdeer, Savannah Sparrow, and Bobolink. With luck you might find a Northern Bobwhite. (Northern Bobwhites in New Hampshire, however, are most likely re-leased gamebirds.) In 0.4 mile from the marsh, stop near the airplane hangars to look for Cliff and Barn Swallows, which nest in the open hangars.

Turn right, opposite the hangars, and go 0.3 mile to a swamp on the left. Check the swamp for American Bittern and Northern Waterthrush. Continue for 0.1 mile to a spruce/fir stand. If you "pish" here, you may coax out Golden-crowned Kinglet, Nashville Warbler, and White-throated Sparrow.

Turn around and return to the junction of Airport and Hazen Roads. Turn left onto Colby Road (unmarked) and go 1.5 miles to U.S. Highway 3. As you drive along Colby Road, breathe deeply and enjoy the sun-baked balsam fragrance from the fir trees along both sides of the road. Turn left on U.S. Highway 3, and in 6.6 miles you will come to U.S. Highway 302 in Twin Mountain. To return to Franconia Notch, continue south on U.S. Highway 3. To reach Crawford Notch turn left and go east on U.S. Highway 302.

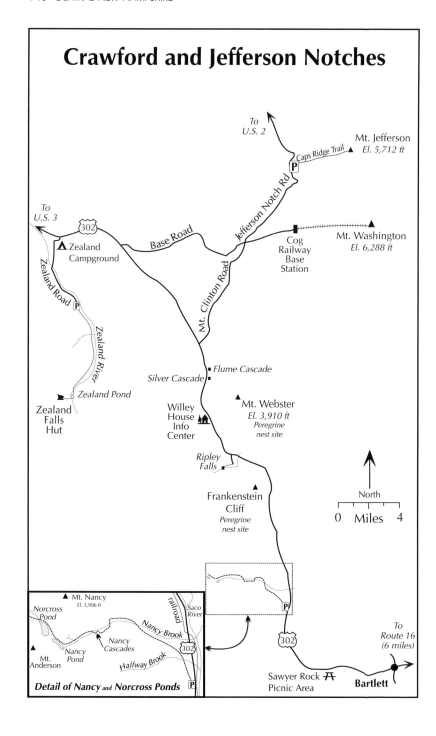

Crawford and Jefferson Notches

To U.S. 2

Caps Ridge Trail

P

Mt. Jefferson
El. 5,712 ft

To U.S. 3

302

Base Road

Jefferson Notch Rd

Mt. Washington
El. 6,288 ft

Cog Railway Base Station

Zealand Campground

Zealand Road

P

Zealand River

Mt. Clinton Road

Zealand Pond

Zealand Falls Hut

Flume Cascade

Silver Cascade

Willey House Info Center

Mt. Webster
El. 3,910 ft
Peregrine nest site

Ripley Falls

North

0   Miles   4

Frankenstein Cliff
Peregrine nest site

Mt. Nancy
El. 3,906 ft

Norcross Pond

railroad

Saco River

Nancy Brook

Mt. Anderson

Nancy Pond

Nancy Cascades

302

Halfway Brook

P

Detail of Nancy and Norcross Ponds

P

302

Sawyer Rock Picnic Area

Bartlett

To Route 16 (6 miles)

Q. CRAWFORD AND JEFFERSON NOTCHES

This trip starts at the junction of State Route 16 and U.S. Highway 302, between North Conway and Jackson, taking you on a tour through Crawford and Jefferson Notches. The scenery in Crawford Notch is as rewarding as the birding. There are numerous facilities for lodging in North Conway and Jackson along State Route 16, plus restaurants, stores, and gas stations. You can find campgrounds in Bartlett (on U.S. Highway 302) and in Crawford Notch State Park. Spring, summer, and fall are fruitful times for this trip, although June may be the best time of all to find boreal birds during nesting season. *Allow one to two days for this trip, depending on how much hiking you plan to do.*

Nancy Pond Trail

From the junction of State Route 16 and U.S. Highway 302 just south of Jackson, follow U.S. Highway 302 west for 11.1 miles to the Nancy Pond Trail Head on the left side of the road. There is a gravel parking area on the edge of the road and a small brown sign.

The Nancy Pond Trail is a productive hike for many boreal specialties, including Spruce Grouse, Black-backed Woodpecker, Bicknell's and Swainson's Thrushes, Philadelphia Vireo, and Rusty Blackbird. This trail is one of the better nesting locations in New Hampshire for the local and rare Three-toed Woodpecker.

The Spruce Grouse and Black-backed Woodpecker are uncommon year-round residents of the boreal forest. The Three-toed Woodpecker is rare in the state, often going several years between sightings. Bicknell's Thrush is fairly common at elevations above 3,000 feet, where it is most easily located by song. Philadelphia Vireo is also fairly common but should be seen to be identified, since its song may be easily confused with those of Solitary and Red-eyed Vireos. Rusty Blackbird is a fairly common breeder in the boreal swamps and bogs.

This is a moderately strenuous hike, starting out at 1,000 feet above sea level, that will take you nearly 4 miles (one way) with a 2,100-foot climb in elevation. Yellow blazes mark the trail through any confusing places, and it follows old roads in other places. You should allow 4 to 5 hours for the round trip hike, plus time for birding. *Be sure to carry drinking water, and be mindful of the weather because it can change very rapidly in the mountains.*

Black-backed Woodpecker
Georges Dremeaux

The best time to hike this trail is in June, to catch the peak of the nesting season. Near the start of the trail, at lower elevations, you should find such species as Red-breasted and White-breasted Nuthatches, Yellow-throated Vireo, Pine Warbler, and Scarlet Tanager. Farther up the trail look for Yellow-bellied Sapsucker, Winter Wren, Golden-crowned Kinglet, and Black-throated Blue, Blackburnian, Bay-breasted, and Blackpoll Warblers. If you can be the first person on the trail in the morning, you will greatly improve your chances of finding something interesting.

As you hike the trail, the 2.2-mile mark will bring you to Nancy Cascade. The section just beyond the cascade is a likely area for Spruce Grouse. The grouse can be terribly unpredictable—sometimes easy to find, sometimes impossible. This bird will often sit perfectly still in a spruce tree, blending in so well that even experienced birders will miss it. Sometimes encountering a hen and her brood is possible in late June and July. About 0.5 mile beyond the cascade you will enter a stand of spruce trees. Listen carefully here for any pecking sounds, since this is the best area for the elusive Three-toed Woodpecker.

Another 0.5 mile will bring you to Nancy Pond, where you should find Black-backed Woodpecker and Rusty Blackbird. An additional 0.5 mile will lead you to Norcross Pond, another reliable spot for Black-backed Woodpecker and Rusty Blackbird.

In the vicinity of both Nancy and Norcross Ponds you are at an elevation of 3,100 feet. At this altitude you should listen for the song of a Bicknell's Thrush. From Norcross Pond return to your car for a well-deserved rest.

Crawford Notch State Park

There are many scenic vistas and breathtaking views in Crawford Notch State Park. U.S. Highway 302 passes through the notch at a maximum elevation of 1,773 feet. In the late 19th and early 20th centuries, Crawford Notch was a popular base of operations for ornithologists working in the White Mountains. One of those working from this base was Bradford Torrey. During the summers Torrey would take the train from Boston to Crawford Notch; he would post himself at the Crawford House and make regular bird forays into the White Mountains.

From the Nancy Pond Trail Head, continue northwest along U.S. Highway 302 for 5.4 miles to a road on the left that leads 0.3 mile to the Ripley Falls Trail Head. A 20-minute hike will take you to the falls. This area is not noted for birds, but you should pick up Veery, Pine and Black-and-white Warblers, and Rose-breasted Grosbeak. Besides, the falls are certainly picturesque.

Return to U.S. Highway 302 and continue for 1.0 mile to the Willey House historic area, where you will find a park information center, restrooms, snack bar, and gift shop. In 1825 Samuel Willey, Jr., settled here, where his family subsequently operated an inn. The next year amid floods and mudslides in the mountains the family perished, while their inn remained curiously undamaged.

Peregrine Falcons nest on the cliffs in the Crawford Notch area. From the late 1970s through the early 1980s more than 30 young Peregrine Falcons were released at historic nest sites in the state. The Crawford Notch area usually has one of several active eyries in the White Mountains. Inquire at the park information center for current nesting sites, or watch for the Audubon Society of New Hampshire volunteers monitoring the sites from the roadside from April through June. You will need a spotting scope to see the birds because the nest sites are high above the road on the towering cliffs.

Philadelphia Vireo
Shawneen E. Finnegan

Continuing on U.S. Highway 302 for 1.8 miles you will come to the parking area for Silver Cascade; in another 0.2 mile is Flume Cascade. These scenic waterfalls are worth a quick stop each.

Zealand Trail

From Flume Cascade continue along U.S. Highway 302 for 6.8 miles to Zealand Road. Turn left and follow Zealand Road uphill for 3.4 miles to the parking lot at the start of the Zealand Trail. The Zealand Trail is a relatively easy hike, starting out at 2,100 feet and rising to 2,700 feet over a distance of 2.7 miles. At the end of the Zealand Trail you will find the Zealand Falls AMC Hut. Both Zealand Road and the trail follow the Zealand River. The trail crosses back and forth over the river a few times. There are sturdy bridges at these river crossings. Allow about 1.5 hours for the one-way hike, or 3 hours for a round trip, plus additional time for birding. The trail is clearly marked with blue blazes.

The Zealand Trail is a productive hike for many boreal species, including such possibilities as Spruce Grouse (rare), Black-backed Woodpecker, Boreal Chickadee, Gray Jay, and Blackpoll, Bay-breasted, Tennessee, and Nashville Warblers. The best time of year to hike this trail for these species is during June.

Near the beginning of the trail there is a short section that is a bit rough and rocky, but it soon smooths out to an easy walk. A little over half way (or about 1.5 miles from the start) you will come to an open meadow alongside the Zealand River. This is the first of several such spots. These open areas are the best locations for such birds as Olive-sided, Yellow-bellied, and Alder Flycatchers, Winter Wren, Philadelphia Vireo, Nashville Warbler, and Purple Finch.

Shortly before the hut you will come to Zealand Pond on the right. The trail skirts around the pond. The last 0.1 mile before the hut is a steep, uphill climb over a rocky slope. Depending on your climbing ability, you may want to skip that section and turn around at the pond.

Jefferson Notch

Return on Zealand Road to U.S. Highway 302, turn right, and backtrack on 302 for 2.2 miles, turning left on Base Road. Follow Base Road for 4.4 miles to a 4-way junction.

At the 4-way junction, if you continue straight and go 1.5 miles, you will come to the Cog Railway Base Station. From here you can take the scenic train ride to the top of 6,288-foot Mount Washington. The Mount Washington Cog Railway was the world's first mountain-climbing cog railway, starting operations in 1869. The train runs from mid-April to early

Mount Washington from the Cog Railway entrance.

Jefferson Notch, typical area to find Bicknell's Thrush.

November, and reservations are strongly recommended. For reservations and information call 800/922-8825, ext 2, or 603/846-5404, ext 2.

For now, turn left onto the gravel Jefferson Notch Road. As you drive along this road, climbing from the 1,800-foot elevation in Crawford Notch to just over 3,000 feet at the peak of Jefferson Notch, you will notice that the forest changes from mixed hardwoods to spruce/fir. In 3.2 miles you will reach the top of the notch and the parking area on the right side of the road for Caps Ridge Trail. This road reaches a higher elevation than any other free public road in New Hampshire.

In recent years a pair of Black-backed Woodpeckers has nested by the edge of the parking lot. Walk around the edge of the parking lot, listening for any drumming sounds. These woodpeckers will nest in either dead or live trees. Listen also for the songs of Yellow-bellied Flycatcher and Swainson's Thrush. If you are observant, you may see a Snowshoe Hare in the small grassy area on the opposite side of the road.

This is one of the easiest spots in New Hampshire to find nesting Bicknell's Thrush, inasmuch as you can drive up above the 3,000-foot level to where they prefer to nest. (For hints on finding and identifying Bicknell's Thrush in New Hampshire, see Chapter 5.) From the parking lot, the trail leads 2.4 miles to the top of 5,712-foot Mount Jefferson. It is worthwhile to hike at least a short distance along the trail to listen for the nasal *seek-a-day-day* of the Boreal Chickadee and to give you additional opportunities to locate a Bicknell's Thrush. You should also find nesting Bay-breasted and Blackpoll Warblers and Dark-eyed Junco. Be sure to listen for the loud song of the tiny Winter Wren, too.

As you leave the trailhead parking lot, turn right to continue along Jefferson Notch Road. If you are watchful, you may catch a glimpse of a Ruffed Grouse crossing the road. During June the adult females often have a train of young following them. In 5.2 miles you will come to a T at a stop-sign. Turn right and go 1.2 miles to Route 2, turn right, and follow Route 2 for 12 miles to return to Route 16. Another alternative from Jefferson Notch is to retrace your route back through Crawford Notch.

Blackpoll Warbler
Barry Van Dusen

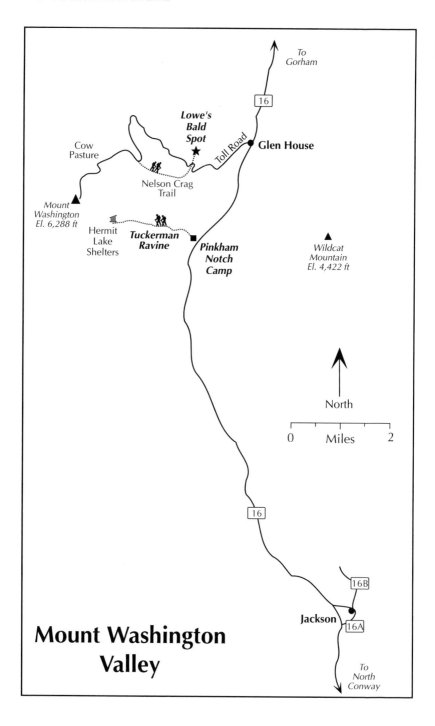

To
Gorham

16

Lowe's
Bald
Spot

Toll Road

Glen House

Cow
Pasture

Nelson Crag
Trail

Mount
Washington
El. 6,288 ft

Hermit
Lake
Shelters

Tuckerman
Ravine

Pinkham
Notch
Camp

Wildcat
Mountain
El. 4,422 ft

North

0   Miles   2

16

16B

Jackson

16A

To
North
Conway

Mount Washington
Valley

R. MOUNT WASHINGTON VALLEY AREA

This section embraces the heart of the White Mountains, a spectacular place. Spring, summer, and fall are all productive times to bird this area. Nesting season in June is especially fruitful. The starting-point for this trip is the town of Jackson, on State Route 16, several miles south of the birding areas in this section. Traveler services such as food, gasoline, and lodging are available in Jackson, and in Gorham to the north, along State Route 16. Besides the birding and the scenery, there are also many other tourist attractions in the area. *Allow 1 to 2 days for this trip, depending on how much hiking you plan to do.*

For tourist information on the Mount Washington Valley area contact:

- Mount Washington Valley Chamber of Commerce
  P.O. Box 2300
  North Conway, NH 03860
  800/367-3364(for lodging reservations)
  603/356-3171(for area information)

For general tourist information on the White Mountain area contact:

- White Mountain Attractions
  P.O. Box 10
  North Woodstock, NH 03262
  603/745-8720
  800/FIND-MTS(from outside NH)

If you are a hiking enthusiast, a good way to start your exploration of this area is with a visit to the Pinkham Notch Camp of the Appalachian Mountain Club (603/466-2725), located along Route 16 in the Mount Washington Valley. This facility serves as a visitor center and also provides relatively inexpensive rustic lodgings and hearty family-style meals for guests. You can obtain up-to-date information on trail conditions and weather at the AMC visitor center, too.

Tuckerman Ravine Trail

The best trail for birding is probably the Tuckerman Ravine Trail which leaves from the Pinkham Notch Camp. This is a fairly rigorous hike and should be undertaken only if you are in top physical condition. The first 2.4 miles of the trail, up to the Hermit Lake shelters, is the easier part. After that, the trail ascends fairly directly to the summit of Mount Washington, and becomes much more difficult. *Remember to keep an eye on the weather when hiking in the mountains, where severe weather can develop rapidly; unwary hikers have died here.*

Birds to look for on the Tuckerman Ravine Trail are typically those of the Canadian Life Zone (boreal forest), including Spruce Grouse, Three-toed (rare) and Black-backed Woodpeckers, Olive-sided and Yellow-bellied Flycatchers, Gray Jay, Boreal Chickadee, Winter Wren, Bicknell's and Swainson's Thrushes, Black-throated Blue, Black-throated Green, Blackburnian, Bay-breasted, Blackpoll, and Canada Warblers, Pine Grosbeak, Red and White-winged Crossbills, and Pine Siskin.

There are also several short, easy hikes in the vicinity of Pinkham Notch. For more information on hiking in the White Mountains contact:

- Pinkham Notch Camp
  Box 298
  Gorham, NH 03581
  603/466-2725 (for trail information)
  603/466-2727 (for reservations)

Mount Washington

There is, of course, Mount Washington itself, the highest peak in the Presidential Range, and in the entire Northeast, reaching 6,288 feet above sea level. The Abenaki called this mountain "Agiocochook" and believed that its summit was the home of the Great Spirit. At one time the mountain was considered too sacred to ascend. Later, the mountain was named for General George Washington in 1784 by the newly independent former British subjects. This occurred after the American Revolution but before George Washington became our first president.

The auto road (fee) that ascends to the top of Mount Washington leaves State Route 16 just 2.5 miles north of the Pinkham Notch Camp. Be forewarned that it is steep, starting out at 1,632 feet above sea level and climbing 4,600 feet in 8 miles. *If you decide to drive up the mountain, make sure that your car is in proper condition.* Be prepared for possible severe weather conditions on the summit—bring a warm sweater or coat, gloves, and hat—at *any* season.

As you ascend Mount Washington, you will discover that the flora changes rapidly. The mixed hardwood forest gives way to Balsam Fir and Red and Black Spruces. Close to timberline, the spruce trees assume a gaunt appearance known as *krummholz*, a German word meaning "twisted wood." Along the way you will encounter some interesting plants, including Five-petaled Diapensia, Labrador Tea, Alpine Azalea, Mountain Avens, Moss Campion, Alpine Goldenrod, and Robbins's Cinquefoil.

As you proceed up the auto road, there are several trail-crossings that permit you to park your car and take a short hike at some of the higher elevations. From just above the 2-mile mark, hiking a quarter-mile on the Madison Gulf Trail will lead you to Lowe's Bald Spot, which affords a fine view of the Presidential Range and Pinkham Notch.

On the opposite side of the road (from the Madison Gulf Trail), follow the Old Jackson Road Trail for 0.2 mile and bear right onto the Nelson Crag Trail. This trail starts out at 2,700 feet above sea level and continues to the top of Mount Washington. However, a relatively short hike along this trail can be productive for birding. From the start of the trail a quarter-mile hike will take you over the 3,000-foot level, the preferred habitat of Bicknell's Thrush. Over the next quarter-mile the trail climbs to 3,500 feet. Familiarizing yourself with the song of Bicknell's Thrush will greatly increase your chances of finding one.

Return to your car and continue your drive up the auto road. In 0.5 mile from the last trailhead stop (the 2.7-mile point), the road rises above the 3,000-foot level. From here to the timberline, remember to listen for Bicknell's Thrush. In recent years, American Pipits have nested at the "Cow Pasture" along the Mount Washington Auto Road at the 6.5-mile mark.

An alternative to driving your own car is to purchase a ride on a van that will whisk you to the top of the mountain and back. The only disadvantage is that you cannot stop wherever the mood strikes you. Another option is to take the Cog Railway to the summit (see section on Jefferson Notch).

From spring through fall, Black Bears are active in the White Mountains. You are most likely to encounter one if you are hiking or camping. If you do see one, remember that they are wild animals and should be treated with caution and respect; an angry bear is a very dangerous beast.

Kancamagus Highway

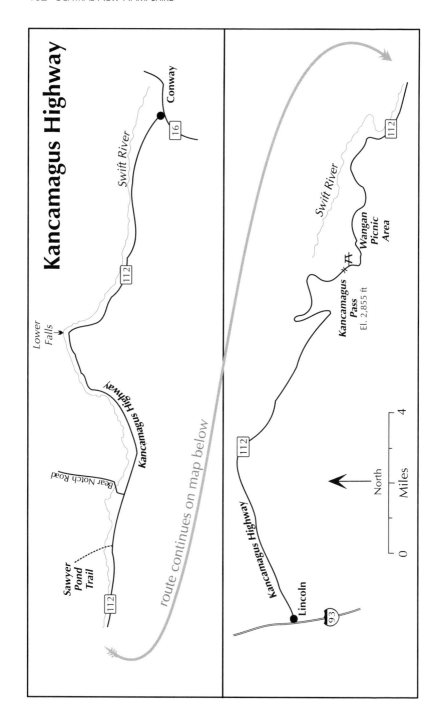

S. KANCAMAGUS HIGHWAY

This side-trip is more for scenery than for birds, although given its location in the White Mountains, anything is possible. The starting-point for this trip is the junction of State Routes 16 and 112 in Conway. The end-point is 34 miles west at the junction with Interstate 93 in Lincoln. This route is rated as one of the most spectacular drives in the eastern U.S.

All traveler services can be found in the towns of Conway and Lincoln at the two end-points. There are several campgrounds along the Kancamagus Highway. No gas stations or other traveler services are available along this 34-mile stretch. Visitor information centers are located at each end in the towns of Conway and Lincoln, respectively.

There are several picnic areas and scenic overlooks along the highway. The junction with Bear Notch Road (which goes off to the north) is a worthwhile spot to stop and look for Red Crossbill and Purple Finch. The Sawyer Pond Trail can be productive for Sharp-shinned and Cooper's Hawks, as well as for both Black-backed and Pileated Woodpeckers. Be sure to stop at the Wangan Picnic Area near Kancamagus Pass, where the highway reaches its highest elevation of 2,855 feet. Keep an eye out for Moose along the edge of the highway.

In Lincoln you can ride the gondola to the top of 3,075-foot Loon Mountain. The gondola operates from late May to mid-October; of course, it is most active during the skiing season. At the top of the mountain you will find an observation tower and a nature trail. Besides the view, you may find a few interesting birds, such as Gray Jay and Boreal Chickadee.

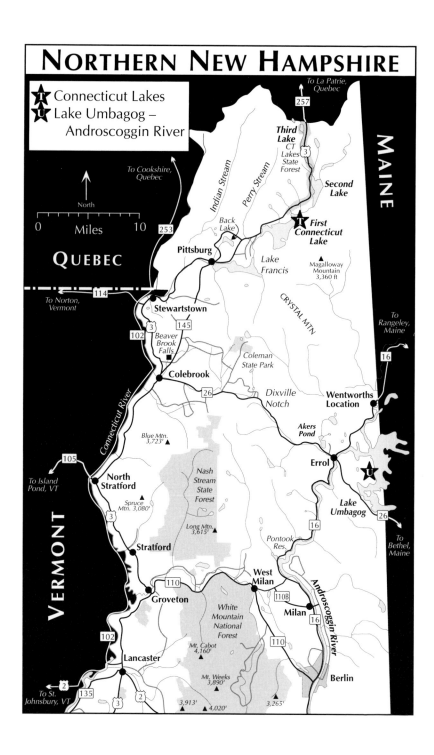

NORTHERN NEW HAMPSHIRE

★ Connecticut Lakes
★ Lake Umbagog – Androscoggin River

To La Patrie, Quebec

257

Third Lake
CT Lakes State Forest

3

Second Lake

To Cookshire, Quebec

North

Miles
0 — 10

253

Back Lake

★ **First Connecticut Lake**

QUEBEC

Pittsburg

Lake Francis

Magalloway Mountain 3,360 ft

CRYSTAL MTN

114

To Norton, Vermont

102 3

Stewartstown

145

Beaver Brook Falls

Colebrook

26

Coleman State Park

Dixville Notch

Wentworths Location

Akers Pond

Errol

★ **U**

To Rangeley, Maine

16

Blue Mtn. 3,723'

105

To Island Pond, VT

North Stratford

3

Spruce Mtn. 3,080'

Nash Stream State Forest

Lake Umbagog

26

To Bethel, Maine

Long Mtn. 3,615'

Stratford

Pontook Res.

16

110

West Milan

110B

Milan

16

Groveton

White Mountain National Forest

Androscoggin River

102

Mt. Cabot 4,160'

Lancaster

Mt. Weeks 3,890'

Berlin

2

135 3 2

To St. Johnsbury, VT

3,913' ▲ 4,020'

3,265'

VERMONT

MAINE

Connecticut River

Chapter 4:

NORTHERN NEW HAMPSHIRE

This section encompasses everything north of the White Mountains to the Canadian border. This area of New Hampshire is the true rural part of the state. The forests become distinctly boreal, and most of the tourists never make it this far north. Much of the land in this region is owned by large paper companies; however, they typically do not post the land but do allow people to travel on their property during daylight hours.

Lincoln's Sparrow
Georges Dremeaux

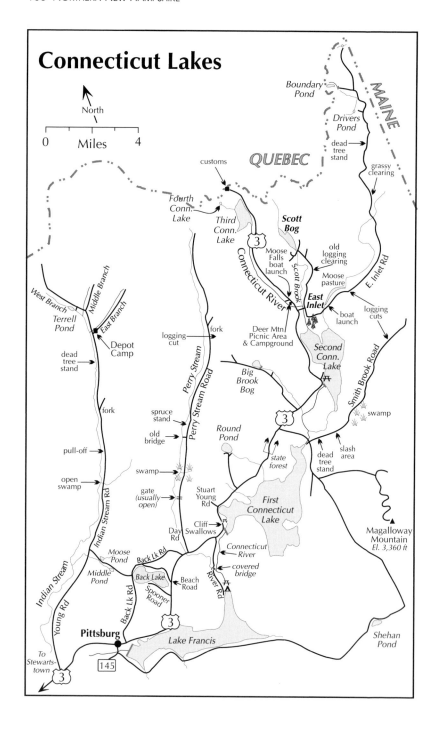

Connecticut Lakes

T. CONNECTICUT LAKES

The Connecticut Lakes area, source of the Connecticut River, provides good year-round birding. In April to May and again in September to October migrating waterfowl move through. During winter there are usually large flocks of "winter finches." Perhaps the best time to visit the Connecticut Lakes of New Hampshire is in June, during the nesting season. This is the most likely time to see many of the boreal species that are specialties of this northern latitude.

To reach the Connecticut Lakes region, follow U.S. Highway 3 north from the White Mountains to the town of Pittsburg. There are many housekeeping cabins, a few motels, and several campgrounds. Most of these are located north of the village of Pittsburg along U.S. Highway 3, some are around Back Lake, and a few are near First Connecticut Lake. (Now, however, this is actually the *second* lake, ever since Lake Francis was created by a large dam.) The village has a few grocery stores, gas stations, and restaurants that serve hearty, home-style, north-country meals. *Plan to take at least two days to explore this area.*

For information on camping and lodging facilities in the area contact:

- North Country Chamber of Commerce
  P.O. Box 1
  Colebrook, NH 03576
  603/237-8939

There are numerous logging roads in Pittsburg, most of which have orange, metal barways at the entrances. If a gate is open, then you may drive along the logging road. If a gate is closed, then you may park your car nearby (do not block the gate) and walk along the road. These are private roads through private property, but the timber companies are generous enough to allow public access to much of their land, so please be considerate and obey signs at all times.

Remember that the logging trucks always have the right-of-way. If you encounter one, you had better get out of the way! These large trucks cannot, and will not, "share" the road with you. You must pull your car as far off the road as possible to make room for them. If you stop to bird an area, be sure to park well off to the edge of the road. Do not leave your car so that it blocks the road. *You are a guest on private property, so please be considerate at all times.*

For our birding tour of the Connecticut Lakes region we will start just south of the village of Pittsburg and work northward along U.S. Highway 3 to the Canadian border. This order is used simply as a convenient organization to the various birding areas. You should feel free to alter the order or to skip some places if you are pressed for time. My personal favorite areas include Indian Stream Road, Perry Stream Road, Smith Brook Road, East Inlet, and Scott Brook Road, locally known as Scott's Bog Road.

Indian Stream Road

This logging road stretches north from U.S. Highway 3 for 12 miles along Indian Stream to Terrell Pond. From the junction of State Route 145 and U.S. Highway 3 in the village of Pittsburg, go south on U.S. Highway 3 for 2.5 miles and turn right on Young Road (unmarked). This dirt road is easy to miss because it is situated between two houses and can easily be mistaken for a driveway. (Shortly before Young Road you will pass a few green highway department sheds on the right.) If you cross Indian Stream on Route 3, then you have missed the road.

At 1.0 mile from U.S. Highway 3 you will drive through a large field that hosts Bobolinks and Savannah Sparrows in June. After another 2.0 miles, where a road goes off to the left, stay straight, as Young Road becomes Indian Stream Road (a private logging road). In another 0.2 mile bear left at the fork and proceed for 1.9 miles to a road on the right that leads to Back Lake Road, locally called Crossover Road. From this junction pass through the gate to continue straight on Indian Stream Road for 1.6 miles to an open swampy area. Along the way, listen for Olive-sided and Alder Flycatchers.

Another 0.8 mile will bring you to a pull-off on the left with a view of the stream. Look here for Spotted Sandpiper. In 0.2 mile stay left at the fork and continue for 0.7 mile to an old logging-cut on the right that usually hosts Mourning Warblers in June. Proceed for 0.9 mile and stay left again at the next fork. The spruce trees just past this fork can hold nesting Bay-breasted Warblers. This area can also produce Philadelphia Vireo. Be sure to check any old logging-cuts, for these produce the right habitat for Mourning Warblers. This species is secretive, usually skulking in the undergrowth, and is more often heard than seen. You will find Mourning Warblers easily, however, if you are familiar with their loud two-part song.

After 2.3 miles (from the last fork) you will arrive at a stand of dead trees on the left. In June 1992 a pair of Black-backed Woodpeckers nested in a dead tree at eye-level, 200 feet from the road.

Proceeding for 1.0 mile more will bring you to a logging camp near Terrell Pond. Turn around here and return to U.S. Highway 3.

Back Lake

Back Lake Road leaves U.S. Highway 3 from the center of Pittsburg, just east of the Information Center, which has restrooms (open only in summer). In 1.1 miles pull off on the right near a stream-crossing. Note the Tamarack trees on your right; these interesting trees are deciduous conifers. Check the marshy area on the opposite side of the road for Olive-sided, Alder, and Least Flycatchers. Cooper's Hawk nests in this area, too.

Just ahead on the left is the town recycling and transfer station. When there was an open dump at this site, Black Bears regularly came at night to pick through the garbage. There are a fair number of Black Bears in the Connecticut Lakes region, and you may encounter one, especially if you are hiking or camping. Remember that you should not attempt to approach these wild, very powerful animals.

Continue along Back Lake Road and in 1.4 miles turn left on an unmarked dirt road, the other end of Crossover Road, cited on the previous page. Drive 0.8 mile and turn left into an access area for Middle Pond. Hooded Mergansers nest here in summer. Listen for Winter Wren, Veery, and Hermit Thrush. You may also see an Osprey fishing over the pond. In another 0.5 mile you will come to Moose Pond on the right. You may find Wood Ducks here. If you continue out this road for another 0.6 mile, you will come to Indian Stream Road. For now, though, return to Back Lake Road.

Turn left (north) on Back Lake Road and go 0.3 mile to a pull-off on the right with a view of the lake. This stop should afford clear scoping during waterfowl migration. The lake is relatively shallow with an average depth of 20 to 30 feet, which provides prime feeding conditions for ducks. In October there can be an impressive buildup of migrating waterfowl, including Red-necked Grebe, many dabblers, and all three scoters. You may also see shorebirds and Bonaparte's Gulls in migration.

Continue for 0.2 mile and stay right at the fork with Beach Road. Another 1.4 miles will bring you to U.S. Highway 3.

During waterfowl migration, the boat-launch on Spooner Road provides another access point to Back Lake that is worth checking. From the point where Beach Road rejoins U.S. Highway 3, go south on Route 3 for 0.6 mile, turn right onto Spooner Road, and go 0.3 mile to the Bacon Boat Launch.

Perry Stream

From the northern junction of Back Lake Road and U.S. Highway 3 (1.0 mile north of the Beach Road/U.S. 3 intersection), go 0.2 mile north on U.S. Highway 3, turning left onto Day Road. In 1.1 miles there will be an open area on your left and a stand of spruce trees on your right. Stop here to check for Lincoln's Sparrow singing from a perch in the clearing. Cape May Warblers are sometimes found in the spruce stand on the right side of the road.

In another mile you will pass through an orange barway gate onto private timber company property. At the gate the name of the road changes to Perry Stream Road. Drive slowly along this dirt road with your windows down and stop wherever you hear birds calling, including several species of warblers. American Redstart is especially common along this stretch. There are numerous stands of dead trees; stop and check them all for Black-backed Woodpecker.

From the gate, proceed 0.7 mile to brushy areas on both sides of the road. Check here for Mourning Warbler and Lincoln's Sparrow. Continue for another 0.1 mile (staying left at the fork) to a loop road on the left, which rejoins Perry Stream Road in 0.2 mile. Drive through the loop road to check for Alder Flycatcher, Winter Wren, Nashville, Magnolia, and Wilson's Warblers, and Northern Parula. Listen for Veery, Swainson's Thrush, and Solitary Vireo. If you are lucky, you may find a Rusty Blackbird here. Rusty Blackbirds prefer to nest in swampy woods, where the males will sing from the treetops. Their song is somewhat reminiscent of that of Red-winged Blackbird but harsher. During nesting season the males appear as a plain blackbird with a yellow eye. Only during autumn do they appear "rusty".

October is an excellent time to find Barred and Great Horned Owls. A Great Gray Owl was found here in the fall of 1968.

From the point where the loop road rejoins Perry Stream Road, continue for 0.9 mile and turn left on a short road to the edge of Perry Stream, where you can see the remains of an old bridge that once crossed the stream. Check for birds similar to those at the previous stop. Listen for the *quick-three-cheers* call of the Olive-sided Flycatcher. In another 0.5 mile you will come to a small stand of spruce trees. Look for Northern Flicker, Boreal Chickadee, and Golden-crowned Kinglet.

Continue for 3.1 miles, stay left at the fork, and proceed another 0.2 mile to an old logging-cut. As mentioned before, Mourning Warblers like these brushy areas formed by the re-growth in logging-cuts. Check this area for Lincoln's Sparrow, also.

In just over 3 miles you will come to a point where the road becomes impassable. Fortunately, there is plenty of room to turn around here. Return to U.S. Highway 3.

Lake Francis

From the junction of Day Road (Perry Stream Road) and U.S. Highway 3, go left (east and then north) on U.S. Highway 3, for 1.1 miles, turning right onto River Road, which leads 2 miles to Lake Francis State Park. Half way to the lake you will come to an old covered bridge (closed to auto traffic) with a new bridge alongside it. Stop by the stream and check for Hairy Woodpecker, Boreal Chickadee, Red-breasted Nuthatch, Ruby-crowned Kinglet, Veery, Swainson's Thrush, Solitary Vireo, Northern Parula, Magnolia Warbler, and American Redstart. This is also a reliable spot for Olive-sided Flycatcher. In 1993 Ospreys started nesting around Lake Francis.

There is a latrine, picnic area, and boat-launch at the state park. The campground is a likely place to find Gray Jays as they scavenge for food.

Even during winter there is usually open water where the Connecticut River flows out of Lake Francis at Murphy Dam. Check the open water in the river for American Black Duck, Mallard, and Hooded and Common Mergansers.

First Connecticut Lake

Return to U.S. Highway 3, turning right to continue north. In 0.4 mile you will come to First Connecticut Lake. Pull in at the picnic area and boat-launch just north of the dam. There is also a chemical toilet here. Be sure to watch for Common Loons, which nest on the Connecticut Lakes.

In spring and summer you should hear Common Snipe and Savannah Sparrow from the grassy area along the shore just north of the dam. Look for Spotted Sandpipers walking along the shoreline in early June. The house on the opposite side of U.S. Highway 3 from the dam has a few nesting Cliff Swallows. (They are more reliably found at the nests on the high school building in "downtown" Pittsburg.)

Continue along U.S. Highway 3 for another 0.9 mile and turn left onto Stuart Young Road. The cabins on the right side of the road have nesting Barn and Cliff Swallows under the eaves. This site thus provides an easy opportunity to compare these two swallow species and the differences in their nest structures. The Barn Swallow's mud nest is built like a small

First Connecticut Lake, where Common Loons nest.

semicircular platter, with the center tapered down, almost cone-shape. The Cliff Swallow's nest is a gourd-shaped structure, with its entrance almost tubular, and built of pellets of mud and clay.

Round Pond

Proceed northeast along U.S. Highway 3 for another 1.0 mile and turn left on an unmarked gravel road that leads to Round Pond. The road starts out climbing steeply uphill. In 1.2 miles the road passes through an orange gate and becomes rougher. In 0.2 mile after the gate, bear left at the fork and stop along the edge of the road to look for Philadelphia Vireo, Northern Parula, and Black-throated Blue Warbler. Identification of the Philadelphia Vireo should be made with care, because to many listeners its song is similar to that of both Solitary and Red-eyed Vireos. Philadelphia Vireo, therefore, really should be seen to make a positive identification, unless you are *very* familiar with this species and its song.

In 0.1 mile from the fork you will come to a public boat-launch on Round Pond. During spring and fall check here for migrant waterfowl. During summer look for Chimney Swifts over the pond if you missed them "downtown." Return to U.S. Highway 3 and continue driving north.

Connecticut Lakes State Forest

As you proceed north along U.S. Highway 3 between the First and Second Connecticut Lakes, stop frequently at the roadside pull-offs. Make sure that your vehicle is all the way off the road, because large logging trucks rumble at considerable speed along U.S. Highway 3. This is a productive stretch for boreal birds nonetheless.

In 1.7 miles north from Round Pond Road you will enter the Connecticut Lakes State Forest and come almost immediately to a large pull-off on the right. The State Forest encompasses a narrow strip along U.S. Highway 3 from this point north to the Canadian border. The section from the pull-off at the top of the hill and continuing down the north slope of the hill to a stream-crossing at the bottom can be especially productive.

Look for Ruffed Grouse, Common Snipe, Yellow-bellied Sapsucker, Black-backed and Pileated Woodpeckers, Olive-sided, Yellow-bellied (uncommon), Alder, and Least Flycatchers, Solitary, Philadelphia, and Red-eyed Vireos, and Tennessee, Black-throated Blue, Black-throated Green, and Mourning Warblers. If you are having a lucky day, you may even see a Northern Goshawk. Winter is the best time to look for Pine Grosbeak and Red and White-winged Crossbills.

You should also notice several wet, muddy areas along the edge of the road that are frequented by Moose. This is the best spot in New Hampshire to obtain a close-up look at a Moose. In fact, the entire stretch of U.S. Highway 3 north of Pittsburg is known locally as "Moose Alley." The tourists come out in force in the early evenings in summer to engage in Moose-watching. It takes little effort to see a dozen or more Moose on any given evening.

Curiously, Woodland Caribou occurred irregularly in the Connecticut Lakes region until early in the 20th century. These animals were probably wanderers from herds in Canada. Some recent attempts to reintroduce Caribou into nearby Maine have met with rather poor success.

Smith Brook Road

From the point on U.S. Highway 3 where the sign indicates the beginning of the state forest, drive north another 1.0 mile and turn right at the sign for the Magalloway Lookout Station. Proceed for 1.1 miles on this gravel road, crossing over Smith Brook on a wooden bridge. Just beyond the bridge, turn left at a 4-way junction and pass through an orange barway gate. This is Smith Brook Road, which runs northeast for about 6 miles. As you drive this road, keep your windows down, and during June you should hear a fairly steady chorus of Winter Wren, Solitary and Red-eyed Vireos, Northern Parula, and White-throated Sparrow.

From the junction go 0.3 mile to a stand of dead trees on the left. Check for Yellow-bellied Sapsucker, Northern Flicker, and Pileated Woodpecker. In another 1.4 miles there will be a cut-over slash area on the left with a fair number of standing dead trees a short distance from the road. Check again for woodpeckers. You may also see a Broad-winged Hawk.

Another 0.6 mile will bring you to a swamp on the right side of the road near a few logging cabins. In June Common Snipe call from the tops of the dead trees. Belted Kingfishers sometimes fish at the swamp, and you may hear a Northern Waterthrush singing. Check the spruce trees for Magnolia Warbler, Dark-eyed Junco, Purple Finch, and Pine Siskin.

Drive another 4.0 miles to a logging cabin next to the road. Along this section listen for Boreal Chickadee, Red-breasted Nuthatch, Brown Creeper, Golden-crowned Kinglet, Swainson's Thrush, Philadelphia Vireo, and Mourning Warbler. Near the cabin look for Purple Finches. Smith Brook Road comes to a dead end in another half mile, so turn around here and return to U.S. Highway 3.

Big Brook Bog

From the junction of U.S. Highway 3 and Magalloway Road (where you turned to access Smith Brook Road), go north onto U.S. Highway 3 for 0.8 mile, turning left on an unmarked logging road that leads to Big Brook Bog. A stand of dead birch trees on the right attracts American Kestrel, Northern Flicker, and Pileated Woodpecker. The road climbs steadily uphill. In 1.7 miles from U.S. Highway 3 stay left at the fork, go another 0.6 mile, turn right, and go 0.1 mile to the dam. During waterfowl migration you may find ducks on the pond above the dam. In summer look and listen for passerines.

Return 0.1 mile to the main logging road. Continuing beyond here the road becomes a little rougher. If your vehicle does not have adequate ground clearance, you should turn left and return to U.S. Highway 3. Otherwise, turn right and continue 1.1 miles to a fork in the road. Stop at the fork and check for wood warblers. Bear left at the fork and go 1.0 mile to where the road dead-ends just short of reaching Perry Stream Road. Turn around here and return to U.S. Highway 3.

Second Connecticut Lake

From the intersection with the road to Big Brook Bog, go north on U.S. Highway 3 for 1.4 miles to the Second Connecticut Lake dam. At the south end of the lake, near the dam, there is a picnic area and a chemical toilet. As you proceed north along U.S. Highway 3, continue to stop at roadside pull-offs to search for any of the boreal species which you may have missed earlier.

East Inlet

Some 3.1 miles north from the Second Lake dam, turn hard right onto an unmarked gravel road immediately after a section of guard rail where U.S. Highway 3 curves left. In 0.3 mile the road crosses a wooden bridge and then comes to a T. Park off to the edge and make a quick check around this intersection. The left, back edge of the intersection area is a reliable spot to find Olive-sided Flycatcher and Rusty Blackbird. Listen, too, for the *chu-wee* call of the Yellow-bellied Flycatcher. You should also hear the ascending whistles of Swainson's Thrush, which can resemble a Hermit Thrush in a hurry.

Turn right at the T, drive 0.4 mile, and pull off by a pair of old roads on the right. Walk out the left road (which is higher and drier) for 100 yards to a junction where the right road rejoins. The spruce trees at this junction often harbor Boreal Chickadees. Listen for their wheezy notes. You should also be able to find Red-breasted Nuthatch, Ruby-crowned Kinglet, and Tennessee (rare), Magnolia, and Blackpoll Warblers.

Return to your car and continue along East Inlet Road for 1.1 miles. Turn left to pull in by the dam and boat-launch at East Inlet. There is a sign indicating that this is a New Hampshire Fish and Game Wildlife Management Area. This is a popular spot with anglers, so try to arrive early in the morning before it becomes too busy. Early morning is also the best time to find Moose feeding on the aquatic plants that grow in this shallow pond.

This is a convenient place to launch a canoe and paddle northeast from the dam for approximately a mile to Moose Pasture. The Moose Pasture area is on the north side of East Inlet pond. Several interesting birds have been recorded here, including Spruce Grouse, the rare Three-toed Woodpecker, Black-backed Woodpecker, Gray Jay, Common Raven, and Lincoln's Sparrow. Common Snipe call from the tops of dead trees along the edge of the inlet, Great Horned Owls nest nearby, and Yellow-bellied Flycatchers can be heard from the surrounding woods.

The spruce forest around East Inlet is perhaps the most reliable area in New Hampshire to find Spruce Grouse.

If you feel up to a 12-mile adventure into the wilderness, turn left as you leave East Inlet and continue driving out East Inlet Road. Stop at any of the stream-crossings and listen for Northern Waterthrush. Gray Jays may be encountered anywhere along this road. In 1.2 miles stop by the brushy area on the left where new growth is reclaiming an old logging-cut. Check for Olive-sided Flycatcher, Nashville, Magnolia, Mourning, and Wilson's Warblers, and Dark-eyed Junco. Scan the dead trees in the distance for Black-backed Woodpecker.

In 4.3 miles you will come to a small grassy clearing on the right side of the road. During a cool day in June 1992, we found a Spruce Grouse sunning himself in the middle of the road at this spot. Ruffed Grouse is much more common here than Spruce Grouse, so if you see a grouse take careful note of its plumage. The male Spruce Grouse has a black throat and breast, whereas the Ruffed Grouse is pale on the front. The field guides show red combs over the male Spruce Grouse's eyes, but these are usually not visible in the field. In both males and females, the eastern race of Spruce Grouse has a dark tail edged with gold, while the Ruffed Grouse has a lightly banded tail with a prominent subterminal dark band. Another field mark to look for is the tuft on the head of the Ruffed Grouse, which is absent on the Spruce Grouse.

Continue for 2.0 miles to an extensive stand of dead trees on the right. Stop and scan the dead trees for woodpeckers. In 1.3 miles turn left and go 0.1 mile to Drivers Pond. The pond is now very grown in, but you may find Yellow-bellied Sapsucker and Black-backed Woodpecker in the dead trees around its edge. Sharp-shinned and Broad-winged Hawks also nest nearby.

Resume your northward course along East Inlet Road, and in 1.1 miles bear left at the fork and go steeply uphill. In 0.8 mile the road is blocked off by boulders. You can walk a half mile from here to Boundary Pond, so named for its proximity to the boundary between the United States and Canada.

Return to East Inlet Road and turn left to take the opposite side of the fork. In 1.6 miles the road comes to a small pond near the three-point boundary of Maine, New Hampshire, and Quebec. This is a likely area in which to find Common Raven. The road is washed out just below the pond, so you must turn around here and return on East Inlet Road to U.S. Highway 3.

Scott Bog

From the wooden bridge near the entrance to East Inlet Road, turn left (north)—away from East Inlet—to follow Scott Brook Road. Go 1.5 miles to a brushy area of new growth in an old logging-clearing and listen for Mourning and Wilson's Warblers. The wet area beyond the brushy clearing sometimes has nesting Rusty Blackbirds in June. Also listen for Alder Flycatcher and Northern Waterthrush.

In 0.5 mile bear left at the fork, go 0.4 mile, and turn left. Follow this road for 0.2 mile, then immediately after crossing over Scott Brook bear right at the fork onto a rough, narrow track. This will lead 0.1 mile to Scott Bog. Unless you have 4-wheel drive, you will probably want to park near the fork and walk the final 0.1 mile (do not block the access road).

You will find a New Hampshire Fish and Game Wildlife Management Area sign next to the dam. This spot attracts fewer people than East Inlet does and is a likely place to find Moose, especially if you arrive early in the morning. Ring-necked Duck nests at the bog, and Olive-sided Flycatcher is a regular here. Check the spruce trees for Blackpoll Warblers. You may also see a Northern Harrier cruising the marsh at the north end of the large pond. In 1995 a pair of American Bitterns nested on one of the swampy islands in this wilderness wetland. After checking for each of these species, return to your car and drive back to U.S. Highway 3.

Deer Mountain Campground

From the point where East Inlet Road leaves U.S. Highway 3, follow U.S. Highway 3 north for 0.6 mile to Deer Mountain Campground and Forest Fire Station. (This area is also known as Moose Falls.) In addition to the campground there are also a few picnic tables where you can have a picnic lunch.

The campground is a fairly reliable place to find Gray Jay and Boreal Chickadee. Black-backed Woodpeckers have also nested in the campground, although infrequently.

Continue north on U.S. Highway 3 for 0.3 mile and turn left on a small rough dirt road that leads a short distance downhill to Moose Falls Flowage, a wide marshy area along the Connecticut River. Northern Waterthrushes are often heard here, as are many of the common landbirds of the region.

Third Connecticut Lake

From Moose Falls Flowage go north on U.S. Highway 3 for 3.1 miles and turn left into the boat-launch on Third Lake. The launch provides a vantage point to look for waterfowl. Look along the shore for Spotted Sandpiper in early June. This is also a serene place to launch a canoe. Since Third Lake is much smaller than First and Second Connecticut Lakes, it does not attract as many power-boats.

Fourth Connecticut Lake

Another mile on U.S. Highway 3 will bring you to the Canadian border. After stopping at the Canadian Customs Station, go 0.1 mile into Canada and turn right into a picnic area with a magnificent scenic view looking far north over the farmlands of the Quebec countryside.

Return to the United States Customs Station (which has restrooms). If you are interested in embarking on the fairly strenuous one-mile hike to reach Fourth Connecticut Lake, ask for a map and directions at the customs station. The trail departs from U.S. Highway 3 adjacent to the customs station and starts out along the clear-cut that marks the border. This hike is not especially productive for birds, although you may find Rusty Blackbird. The lake is really just a small bog with floating peat and Pitcher-plants. This is conservation property; Champion International Corporation donated this 78-acre parcel of land to The Nature Conservancy in 1990. These two acres of pond and four acres of peat-bog constitute the origin of the mighty Connecticut River.

This hike concludes the discussion of the main birding spots in the Connecticut Lakes region. However, there are several more areas to explore if you have extra time and a sense of adventure. These are described in the following sections.

Magalloway Lookout Station

Between First and Second Connecticut Lakes, the road to the Magalloway Lookout Station departs from the east side of U.S. Highway 3; it is the same road that leads to Smith Brook Road. From Route 3, go 1.1 miles, to the 4-way junction, continue straight for another 1.1 miles, and stay left at the fork. In 0.6 mile stay left again at another fork, and in 2.3 miles turn right toward the lookout tower.

From here the road climbs up Magalloway Mountain and becomes much rougher. Your vehicle needs plenty of ground clearance to make this trip. As you drive the final 3 miles to the trailhead for the Magalloway lookout tower, stop at any of the brushy areas of new growth in the old logging-clearings. Look in these clearings for Alder and Least Flycatchers, Warbling Vireo, and Mourning Warbler. Gray Jays nest around the summit of Magalloway Mountain. If you have a picnic lunch, these unwary birds are likely to arrive to look for a handout.

Lake Francis Loop

This trip takes you on a 23-mile loop from the Magalloway Lookout Station Road, through miles of backcountry, past the south side of Lake Francis, and finally back to U.S. Highway 3 in the village of Pittsburg. There are some very rough sections along this loop, so you should undertake it only if your vehicle has adequate ground clearance.

From U.S. Highway 3, take the Magalloway Lookout Station Road for 1.1 miles to the 4-way junction, continue straight for another 1.1 miles, and stay left at the fork. In 0.6 mile bear right at the fork (away from the lookout tower). In 3.5 miles bear right at the fork where the road drops steeply downhill. In another 1.8 miles the road crosses a stream where you should hear Olive-sided Flycatcher.

Shehan Pond will appear on your left in another 2.0 miles. In 1.8 miles after the pond turn right at the T and go 1.1 miles to a scenic view of Lake Francis. In 0.4 mile bear left and continue for 9.5 miles along the south side of Lake Francis to a stop-sign. Go another 0.1 mile to the junction with Route 145, turn right, and in 0.2 mile you will rejoin U.S. Highway 3 in the village of Pittsburg. The birds on this long ride will be about the same as those found along the shorter routes described earlier, but, if you enjoy exploring places which have a good chance of harboring rare plants, mammals, and butterflies as well as birds, this adventure is for you.

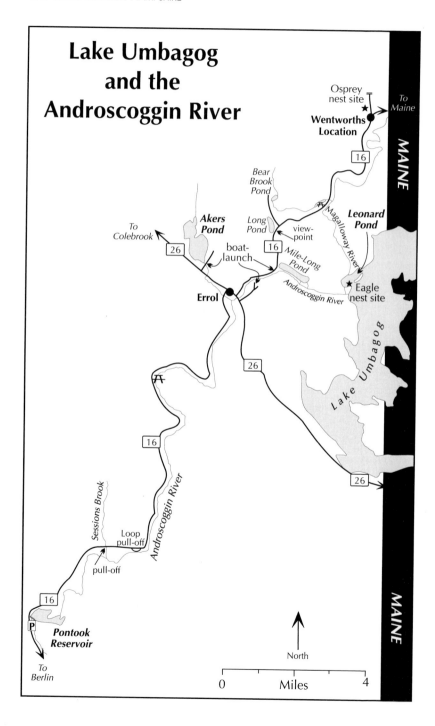

Lake Umbagog and the Androscoggin River

Osprey nest site

To Maine

Wentworths Location

16

MAINE

Bear Brook Pond

Akers Pond

Long Pond

viewpoint

Leonard Pond

To Colebrook

26

boat-launch

16

Mile-Long Pond

Magalloway River

Errol

Androscoggin River

Eagle nest site

26

Lake Umbagog

16

26

Androscoggin River

Sessions Brook

Loop pull-off

pull-off

16

P

Pontook Reservoir

To Berlin

MAINE

North

0   Miles   4

U. LAKE UMBAGOG
AND THE ANDROSCOGGIN RIVER

The headwaters of the Androscoggin River flow out of Lake Umbagog. The lake is mostly in New Hampshire, although about a third of its eastern side is in Maine

This area provides good year-round birding. In April and May, and again in September and October, migrating waterfowl move through. The best time to visit for finding nesting birds is in June. Specialties of this area include nesting Ospreys and Bald Eagles. This is the most reliable area in the state to find these two species during summer. There is not much of a tourist trade around Errol, so a visit in July or August can also be rewarding. Winter is a productive time to visit if one is looking for Boreal Chickadee, Pine Grosbeak, Purple Finch, Red and White-winged Crossbills, Pine Siskin, and Evening Grosbeak. In winter it can be a long, hard drive which can be very bleak.

Accommodations are available in the town of Errol, at the Errol Motel (make reservations) and several camping areas. *Allow a full day to bird this area.*

Pontook Reservoir

From the southern part of the state, take Interstate 93 north to U.S. Highway 3 north, thence to State Route 115 and north to U.S. Highway 2 east, and finally to the town of Gorham. From Gorham follow State Route 16 north along the Androscoggin River for 18 miles, passing through Berlin (BER-lin). Proceeding northward, you will come to the Pontook Reservoir in the town of Dummer. You will find a boat-launch facility and restrooms near the dam.

The reservoir is a good place to start looking for Common Loon, Pied-billed Grebe, American Bittern, Great Blue and Green Herons, American Black and Ring-necked Ducks, Common Goldeneye, Hooded and Common Mergansers, Osprey, Northern Harrier, Common Moorhen, Spotted Sandpiper, Belted Kingfisher, Bank Swallow, and Northern Waterthrush.

Androscoggin River

From the Pontook Reservoir northward, the birding along the Androscoggin River is very productive. Stop frequently as you drive the 15 miles from the reservoir to the town of Errol at the junction of State Routes 16 and 26. Scan the river for waterfowl and watch the sky for Ospreys. Lake Umbagog (um-BAY-gog) and the surrounding area contain New Hampshire's largest concentrations of nesting Ospreys and Common Loons.

In 3.4 miles from the Pontook Reservoir, pull off on the right where Sessions Brook flows into the Androscoggin River. Look for dabbling ducks and for Alder and Least Flycatchers. Continue along State Route 16 for another 1.1 miles to a road on the right that loops in close to the river. This loop shields you from State Route 16 with a buffer of trees between the river and the road. Proceed through the loop to bird this grove and then turn back onto State Route 16.

In 6.1 miles you will come to the Androscoggin State Wayside Picnic Area. This is a pleasant spot for a picnic. Northern Harriers are often encountered in this area. Another 5 miles will bring you to the center of Errol at the junction of State Routes 16 and 26.

Akers Pond

From the junction of State Routes 16 and 26, in the center of Errol, turn left and go west on Route 26 for 1.0 mile. Turn right onto a dirt road and go 0.2 mile to a boat-launch on Akers Pond. Ospreys often fish at this pond.

Return to the center of Errol and follow State Route 26 east for 0.5 mile. Turn left, just after crossing over the Androscoggin River, at the sign reading "To public waters." In 0.4 mile along this road you will see an old logging-cut on the left side of the road with a fair number of standing dead trees. Check for Black-backed Woodpecker and Mourning Warbler in this area.

Continue for 0.2 mile, stay left at the fork, and proceed for 0.3 mile to the paved boat-launch with a large gravel parking area. Scan the river for waterbirds. Return via State Route 26 to the junction with State Route 16 in Errol.

Leonard Pond

From Errol, State Route 16 and the Androscoggin River continue northward toward Lake Umbagog. In 1.5 miles north on State Route 16 from the center of Errol you will find a small gravel boat-launch. A Townsend's Solitaire was seen in the area around the boat-launch several winters ago. This is a good spot to launch a canoe. From this landing,

Bald Eagle
Georges Dremeaux

it is only a short paddle to Leonard Pond, located where the Androscoggin and Magalloway (muh-GAL-o-way) Rivers join with Lake Umbagog.

After an absence of 40 years, Bald Eagles nested in New Hampshire in the spring of 1989. The site which they selected is a large White Pine on an island in Leonard Pond near Lake Umbagog. The eagles have continued to nest here in successive years. The immediate area around the nest tree is roped off to prevent overzealous people from disturbing them. You should have an excellent view of the eagles from well outside the restricted area. Incubation here begins in mid-April, and hatching is in mid-May. The young spend ten weeks in the nest, with fledging occurring in late July or early August. This continues to be the only known Bald Eagle nesting site in the state.

While you are here, check around for other good birds. For example, in June 1990 a Black Tern was seen here.

In 0.2 mile from the boat-launch you will come to Mile Long Pond (along the edge of the Androscoggin River). A Prothonotary Warbler was seen in this area several years ago. Check the pond for waterfowl, such as Ring-necked Ducks.

Long Pond

After Leonard Pond, proceed for 1.0 mile and turn left onto a dirt road that leads a short distance downhill to the edge of Long Pond. This is a productive stop for waterfowl. You may also see Ospreys soaring over the pond in search of fish. The surrounding trees should hold Red-breasted Nuthatch, Winter Wren, Golden-crowned Kinglet, Red-eyed Vireo, Northern Parula, Black-throated Blue Warbler, and White-throated Sparrow.

Bear Brook Pond

Continue north along State Route 16 for 0.2 mile and turn left onto an unmarked logging road that is owned by the Boise Cascade Company. Go 1.0 mile to Bear Brook Pond. Listen for Olive-sided Flycatcher and wood warblers. The road continues beyond the pond but does not lead to any especially productive habitat. Turn around at the pond and return to State Route 16.

Proceed north on State Route 16 for 1.7 miles and turn left into a picnic area alongside a pond formed by Bear Brook where it flows under the road into the Magalloway River. Northern Waterthrushes nest along the edge of the pond.

The section along State Route 16 between the last two stops is prime Moose habitat. Watch along the edge of the road for the low, wet, muddy areas that the Moose enjoy. One of the best spots is the half-mile stretch just after the "Moose Crossing" sign. On weekend nights you may see several cars along this section of State Route 16 with loads of tourists watching for Moose. The Moose will come out to the edge of the road at dusk. Road salt, spread during the winter for improved traction, collects in muddy pools at the edge of the road and attracts the Moose.

Wentworths Location

From the picnic area, continue north on State Route 16 for 3.7 miles and turn left onto an unmarked gravel road just before the Wentworths Location Cemetery. On your left you will notice Mount Dustin, where Golden Eagles have occasionally been seen. Continuing out the gravel road for 0.3 mile you will see an Osprey nest atop a dead tree on the left side of the road. This has been an active nest site for the past several years.

Return to State Route 16 and turn right to return to Errol. If you go any farther north on State Route 16, you will cross into Maine as the road veers northeast.

You may encounter Black Bear in this area, especially if you are hiking or camping. If you see one, remember to treat it with caution, respect, and a healthy skepticism of its motives.

Dixville Notch

If you have a little extra time, you may want to take a scenic side-trip from Errol to Dixville Notch. From the junction of State Routes 16 and 26 in Errol, follow State Route 26 west for 9.4 miles to Dixville Notch State Park. There are a few scenic stops along State Route 26 as you proceed through the park. Peregrine Falcons nest on the cliffs on Abenaki Mountain behind The Balsams Resort, which is located just west of the state park. You should also see most of the regular North Country birds cited in other sections.

Lake Umbagog National Wildlife Refuge

Planning began in 1990 to establish the Lake Umbagog National Wildlife Refuge. The plan is to purchase 7,256 acres that will be the core of the refuge. Conservation easements will be sought on an additional 8,609 acres as a buffer zone, bringing the planned total protected area to 15,865 acres. Since this land was previously in the hands of timber companies that allowed public access to their property, land-use changes will be minimal. What the refuge will accomplish is to protect and preserve this pristine area from the mounting pressures to sell, subdivide, and develop land around the lake.

The majority of the western shore of Lake Umbagog will become part of the refuge, including the previously mentioned Leonard Pond Bald Eagle nest site. As of this writing, the refuge is still in the process of acquiring lands within the planned refuge boundary. The land encompassed by the refuge is open to passive public use at this time.

You can stop by and visit the headquarters at Route 16 North at the Old Brown Owl Store. For more information contact the refuge office at:

- Lake Umbagog National Wildlife Refuge
  P.O. Box 280
  Errol, NH 03579
  603/482-3415

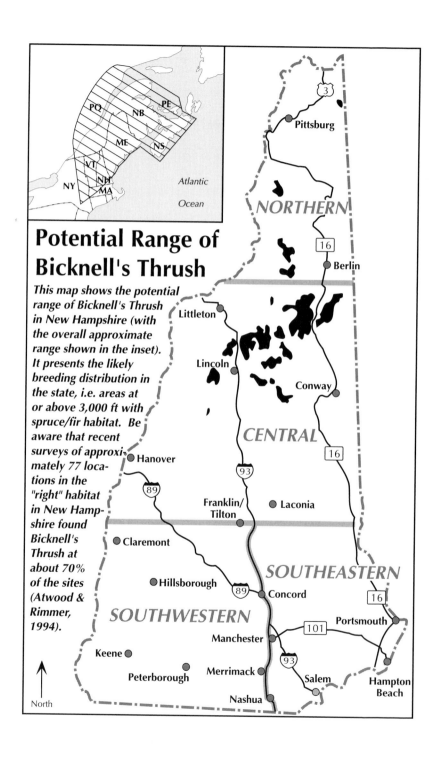

Potential Range of Bicknell's Thrush

This map shows the potential range of Bicknell's Thrush in New Hampshire (with the overall approximate range shown in the inset). It presents the likely breeding distribution in the state, i.e. areas at or above 3,000 ft with spruce/fir habitat. Be aware that recent surveys of approximately 77 locations in the "right" habitat in New Hampshire found Bicknell's Thrush at about 70% of the sites (Atwood & Rimmer, 1994).

NORTHERN

CENTRAL

SOUTHEASTERN

SOUTHWESTERN

Pittsburg

Berlin

Littleton

Lincoln

Conway

Hanover

Franklin/ Tilton

Laconia

Claremont

Hillsborough

Concord

Portsmouth

Keene

Manchester

Merrimack

Salem

Peterborough

Nashua

Hampton Beach

North

Chapter 5:
SOME NOTES ON BICKNELL'S THRUSH

SPECIES STATUS

Bicknell's Thrush was first recognized as a species in 1881 when Eugene P. Bicknell discovered it breeding in the Catskill Mountains of New York. In the American Ornithologists' Union fifth edition of the checklist of North American Birds (1957), Bicknell's Thrush *(Catharus minimus bicknelli)* was listed as a subspecies of Gray-cheeked Thrush. However, recent work by Ouellet (1993) confirms earlier research and has led to the re-separation of two forms of Gray-cheeked Thrush *(minimus* and *bicknelli)* into two separate species. The *minimus* form retains the name Gray-cheeked Thrush, while the *bicknelli* form has again acquired the name Bicknell's Thrush. With the publication of the July 1995 issue of *The Auk,* the AOU splits the two sibling species.

The recent split of these two forms into two separate species: Bicknell's Thrush *(Catharus bicknelli)* and Gray-cheeked Thrush *(Catharus minimus)* will afford those birding in New Hampshire the opportunity to see the "new" Bicknell's Thrush, the Northeast's only endemic songbird. Naturally, this leads to questions on how to locate and identify Bicknell's Thrush. This chapter will briefly cover species status, current range and habitat, identification by sight and song, and breeding biology.

RANGE AND HABITAT

Gray-cheeked Thrush is far more widespread than Bicknell's, its breeding range extending from Newfoundland across northern Canada to southwestern Alaska and into northeastern Siberia. Bicknell's Thrush breeding range is restricted to southern Quebec, the Maritime Provinces, and the higher elevations of New York, Vermont, New Hampshire, and Maine (Wallace 1939, Ouellet 1993, Rimmer in press).

Bicknell's preferred nesting habitat is considered to be dense coniferous forest consisting primarily of Balsam Fir and Red Spruce (Wallace

1939). In New Hampshire this habitat is most readily found at elevations above 3,000 feet in the White Mountains. These are usually on wind-swept slopes (Atwood and Rimmer 1994). A number of the sites are described in the previous text in this book, and a map of likely habitat in New Hampshire is provided at the beginning of this chapter.

Some of these sites that appear in the previous birdfinding chapters of this text are as follows: Franconia Notch,, Nancy Pond Trail, Jefferson Notch, and Mount Washington. The breeding range in the state is almost entirely restricted to the White Mountains proper. In New Hampshire, Bicknell's Thrush appears to have disappeared from Monadnock, Sunapee, and Dixville Notch (Foss 1995).

Recent die-back of Red Spruce, most probably due to atmospheric pollution—and found primarily on western slopes—as well as development of ski resorts in New England, threatens the habitat of the Bicknell's Thrush. Banding studies and other population research suggests, in fact, that Bicknell's Thrush is about as close to being an endangered species as one can get.

On migration in New Hampshire, Bicknell's and Gray-cheeked Thrushes overlap during the last third of May and again during September.

The wintering ranges of the two sibling species do not overlap. Bicknell's winters in Haiti, the Dominican Republic, and possibly Puerto Rico (Rimmer et al. 1993). Gray-cheeks, on the other hand, winter in mainland South and Central Americas (Rimmer et al. 1993).

IDENTIFICATION

According to George John Wallace's treatment in Bent (1949), the only similar species that shares its summer range with Bicknell's is Swainson's Thrush. The altitude range of these two birds overlaps slightly at around the 3,000-foot level. The buffier-toned appearance of the Swainson's head is a good field mark, contrasting with the gray cheek of the Bicknell's Thrush. The light-colored eye-ring of the Swainson's, when visible, is diagnostic (Bent 1949).

The most characteristic call of Swainson's Thrush is a weak, high-pitched *pip*, quite different from Bicknell's sharp, harsh call; and the ascending spirals of Swainson's song do not resemble Bicknell's ringing, more or less even-pitched refrain (Bent 1949). To me, the song of Swainson's is similar to that of the Hermit Thrush, but sounds as if the bird is in a hurry to finish the song.

During migration (in late May and in September) you may encounter both Bicknell's and Gray-cheeked Thrushes in New Hampshire (and

b. van dusen

Bicknell's Thrush
Barry W. Van Dusen

throughout New England). Bicknell's is typically a richer (warmer) brown above than Gray-cheeked, which is more olive-gray (Rimmer et al. 1993). Bicknell's tail is a dull chestnut color contrasting with the browner back, as opposed to the Gray-cheek's tail, which is olive-colored and does not contrast with the back (Ouellet 1993, Rimmer et al. 1993). The pale area at the base of the lower mandible is extensive and distinctly yellowish in Bicknell's, but smaller and dull fleshy-pink (or yellowish-flesh) in Gray-cheeked (Rimmer et al. 1993).

These are subtle differences, often *very* difficult to discern in the field. And just when you thought it was safe to venture out into the field, more complications come into play. Some observers have indicated that Bicknell's from the Gaspé Peninsula lack the relatively bright yellow on the lower mandible. Also, some Newfoundland Gray-cheeked Thrushes, known to have more extensively pale mandibles and warmer plumage tones, may also appear to have chestnut tails.

According to Wallace's treatment in Bent (1949), Bicknell's is a smaller bird than Gray-cheeked. Certainly, Swainson's Thrush makes a good standard for comparison, being larger than Bicknell's but smaller than Gray-cheeked. But how many times will you see these birds together? These size differences may be useful in the hand, but not necessarily in the field.

Vocalizations of Bicknell's and Gray-cheeked also differ; Bicknell's song is similar to that of a Veery but with a break in the middle of the song and a rising inflection at the end. To my ears it also sounds higher-pitched and faster than that of Gray-cheeked. The song may be represented as *chook-chook, wee-o, wee-o, wee-o-ti-t-ter-ee* (Bent 1949).

The Gray-cheeked lacks the break and rising inflection that are characteristic of Bicknell's song (Bent 1949). Gray-cheeked Thrushes have been characterized as having a more "jumbled" song than Bicknell's (McLaren 1994). To me, the Gray-cheeked sounds as if it starts and stops several times, very disjointedly. It also seems to have a lower-pitched voice and moves through its song more slowly.

The most characteristic call-note of Bicknell's Thrush is a harsh, penetrating, slurred whistle, similar to but harsher and higher-pitched than the familiar *wheu* of the Veery. At times it approaches the sharply whistled call of the Red-winged Blackbird (Bent 1949). The nocturnal flight call of the sibling species have been described as follows: *cree-ee* in Bicknell's and *re-i-i-i-r* or *whe-err* in Gray-cheeked Thrush. Just to complicate things further, Veit and Petersen (1993) say that the "call uttered by nocturnally migrating Gray-cheeked Thrushes is very similar to that of Veery and Rose-breasted Grosbeak, so reports of night-calling migrants must be evaluated with caution."

The best time of year in which to locate a Bicknell's Thrush by voice is from June 1 to 20 when the birds are most vocal, singing consistently throughout the day (Atwood and Rimmer 1994). From late June through mid-September Bicknell's Thrush is more likely to vocalize only at sunrise and sunset.

The chart below summarizes the general identification details to help distinguish Bicknell's Thrush from Gray-cheeked Thrush.

	Bicknell's Thrush	Gray-cheeked Thrush
size	Smaller than Swainson's Thrush	Larger than Swainson's Thrush
nocturnal flight song	Higher *cree-ee*	Lower *pe-i-i-i-r* or *whe-err*
song	Like that of Veery, but faster and higher-pitched. *Chook-chook, wee-o, wee-o, wee-o-ti-t-ter-ee.* Ends in even or ascending pitch.	Jumbled. Lacks break and rising inflection of Bicknell's. Ends in descending pitch.
bill	Pale yellow at base of lower mandible.	Smaller portion of lower mandible is fleshy-pink or yellowish-flesh.
back color	Approaching warm brown	Olive-gray
tail	Usually dull chestnut; contrasts with the browner back	Usually olive; showing little contrast with the back

BREEDING BIOLOGY OF BICKNELL'S THRUSH

Bicknell's Thrush breeds in New England in spruce/fir habitat, usually above 3,000 feet. If the preceding section on identification perplexed you, the clearest way to cinch your identification of a Bicknell's Thrush is to *find it on territory.*

It nests in a small or medium-sized evergreen (usually a Balsam Fir or a Red Spruce, though sometimes in a Paper Birch) near the ground where two or more horizontal branches join the main stem. (See the photo on the back cover.) The nest is usually found 3 to 12 feet off the ground, but sometimes as high as 25 feet. The nest is a cup of distinctive conifer twigs and fresh green moss, with the minor addition of nonconiferous twigs, flower stalks, fern stems, dried leaves, bark, and occasionally lichens. An inner lining for the nest is filled with partially decomposed organic debris and a lining of fine black rootlets with some occasional dry grasses or leaves (Wallace 1939, Bent 1949, Ouellet 1993).

The breeding season begins in late May and extends into late July. A single brood of 3 to 4 eggs is the norm. The eggs are bluish-green, variably spotted with brown. Incubation is by the female alone for a length of 13 to 14 days. The nestlings are altricial and downy, and are tended by both parents. Young Bicknell's Thrushes will leave the nest after 12 to 14 days (Wallace 1939, Bent 1949).

Birders, of course, will be seeking out Bicknell's Thrush in breeding season at the appropriate habitat in New Hampshire. While doing so, however, be careful not to approach active nests or otherwise disturb the birds. While currently not an officially endangered species, Bicknell's Thrush has a fragile hold on its particular habitat in the Northeast and we should all work to ensure the continued survival of this fascinating bird.

RECOMMENDED READINGS ON BICKNELL'S THRUSH

Atwood, J. L., and C. C. Rimmer. 1994. Status and Biology of Bicknell's Thrush in the Northeastern U.S. Manomet Observatory for Conservation Sciences and Vermont Institute of Natural Science.

Bent, A. C. 1949. *Life Histories of North American Thrushes, Kinglets, and their Allies.* Smithsonian Institution.

Foss, C. R. (ed.) 1995. *Atlas of Breeding Birds in New Hampshire.* Audubon Society of New Hampshire/Arcadia.

McLaren, I. 1994. A "New" Species of Thrush? *Nova Scotia Birds* 36(3): 25-26.

McLaren, I. 1995. Field Identification and Taxonomy of Bicknell's Thrush. *Birding* 27(5):358-366.

Ouellet, H. 1993. Bicknell's Thrush: taxonomic status and distribution. *Wilson Bull.* 105:545-572.

Rimmer, C. C., J. L. Atwood, and L. R. Nagy. 1993. Bicknell's Thrush: A Northeastern Songbird in trouble? *Bird Observer* 21(2):84-89.

Rimmer, C. C. 1996. A Closer Look: Bicknell's Thrush. *Birding* in press.

Veit, R., and W. Petersen. 1993. *Birds of Massachusetts.* Massachusetts Audubon Society.

Wallace, G. J. 1939. Bicknell's Thrush, its taxonomy, distribution, and life history. *Proc. Boston Soc. Nat. Hist.* 41:211-402.

Chapter 6:

WHERE TO FIND ADDITIONAL INFORMATION

The addresses and telephone numbers listed in this short chapter should provide you with additional sources of information to help you in birding New Hampshire.

For details on field trips and general information from the Audubon Society of New Hampshire, contact:

- Audubon Society of New Hampshire
  3 Silk Farm Road
  Concord, NH 03301
  603/224-9909

You should know that the ASNH Rare Bird Alert's number is 603/224-9900. The quarterly *New Hampshire Bird Records* is available by subscription ($10 members, $15 non-members, with all renewals taking place annually in October).

- The Seacoast Science Center
  (at Odiorne Point State Park)
  P.O. Box 674, Route 1A
  Rye, NH 03870
  603/436-8043

- The Loon Preservation Committee
  P.O. Box 604
  Moultonborough, NH 03254
  603/476-5666

- Paradise Point Nature Center
  North Shore Road
  East Hebron, NH 03232
  603/744-3516

Government agencies that may be of assistance:

- State of NH Fish and Game Department
  2 Hazen Drive
  Concord, NH 03301
  603/271-3421

- NH Division of Parks and Recreation
  P.O. Box 856
  Concord, NH 03302-0856
  603/271-3254

- NH Office of Vacation Travel
  P.O. Box 856
  Concord, NH 03302-0856
  603/271-2666

- Forest Supervisor
  P.O. Box 638
  Laconia, NH 03247
  603/528-8721

- National Wildlife Refuges - Region V
  One Gateway Center, Suite 700
  Newton Corner, MA 02158

- Great Bay National Wildlife Refuge
  336 Nimble Hill Road
  Newington, NH 03801
  603/431-7511

- Lake Umbagog National Wildlife Refuge
  P.O. Box 280
  Errol, NH 03579
  603/482-3415

Other non-governmental organizations include:

- The Nature Conservancy - NH Field Office
  7 South State Street, Suite 1
  Concord, NH 03301
  603/224-5853

- NH Campground Owners' Association
  P.O. Box 320
  Twin Mountain, NH 03595
  603/846-5511

- Pinkham Notch Camp
  Appalachian Mountain Club
  Box 298
  Gorham, NH 03581
  603/466-2725 for trail information
  603/466-2727 for reservations

- Appalachian Mountain Club
  5 Joy Street
  Boston, MA 02108
  617/523-0636

- Society for the Protection of New Hampshire Forests
  54 Portsmouth Street
  Concord, NH 03301
  603/224-9945

Members of the American Birding Association receive an ABA membership directory which includes a list of New Hampshire residents willing to help visiting birders:

- American Birding Association
  P.O. Box 6599
  Colorado Springs, CO 80934-6599
  800/634-7736 (sales)
  800/850-2473 (membership)

Spruce Grouse
Georges Dremeaux

Chapter 7:

BIRDS OF
NEW HAMPSHIRE

BAR-GRAPHS

The bar-graphs which follow are not intended to show abundance of the bird species, such as a standard checklist does. Rather, these bar-graphs are intended to reflect the *likelihood* of seeing or hearing a bird, rather than its actual numerical *abundance*. The thicker the line, the greater the likelihood of seeing or hearing the bird, providing that you are in the proper habitat at the correct season. There are 342 species listed.

Species which are known to breed in New Hampshire are marked by a star after the species name.

If you find a bird which you believe is unusual (for example, the rarest two categories on the bar-graphs, a new breeding record, or a species that is not in the bar-graphs at all), take careful notes and report your findings as follows: Send written reports to ASNH at their Concord address (marked "attention: New Hampshire Bird Records"). These records are passed on to the sub-regional editors of *National Audubon Society Field Notes* and to the State Records Committee. Sightings of rarities should also be reported to the statewide Rare Bird Alert at 603/224-9900 and, if possible, to the author at 603/887-4681.

▬▬▬▬▬▬▬	Hard to Miss (nearly every trip)
▬▬▬▬▬▬	Should See (3 out of 4 trips)
═══════	May See (1 out of 4 trips)
═══════	Lucky to Find (1 out of 10 trips)
───────	How Lucky can you get (infrequent)
··············	Irregular (sporadic/erratic)

✓	BREEDING?	January	February	March	April	May	June	July	August	September	October	November	December
Red-throated Loon													
Pacific Loon													
Common Loon	★												
Pied-billed Grebe	★												
Horned Grebe													
Red-necked Grebe													
Western Grebe													
Northern Fulmar													
Cory's Shearwater													
Greater Shearwater													
Sooty Shearwater													
Manx Shearwater													
Wilson's Storm-Petrel													
Leach's Storm-Petrel													
Northern Gannet													
Great Cormorant													
Double-crested Cormorant	★												
American Bittern	★												
Least Bittern	★												
Great Blue Heron	★												
Great Egret													
Snowy Egret													
Little Blue Heron													
Tricolored Heron													
Cattle Egret													
Green Heron	★												
Black-crowned Night-Heron	★												
Yellow-crowned Night-Heron													

✓	BREEDING?	January	February	March	April	May	June	July	August	September	October	November	December
Glossy Ibis													
Tundra Swan													
Mute Swan	★												
Gr. White-fronted Goose													
Snow Goose													
Brant													
Canada Goose	★												
Wood Duck	★												
Green-winged Teal	★												
American Black Duck	★												
Mallard	★												
Northern Pintail													
Blue-winged Teal	★												
Northern Shoveler													
Gadwall													
Eurasian Wigeon													
American Wigeon													
Canvasback													
Redhead													
Ring-necked Duck	★												
Greater Scaup													
Lesser Scaup													
Common Eider	★												
King Eider													
Harlequin Duck													
Oldsquaw													
Black Scoter													
Surf Scoter													

✓	BREEDING?	January	February	March	April	May	June	July	August	September	October	November	December
☐ White-winged Scoter													
☐ Common Goldeneye	★												
☐ Barrow's Goldeneye													
☐ Bufflehead													
☐ Hooded Merganser	★												
☐ Common Merganser	★												
☐ Red-breasted Merganser													
☐ Ruddy Duck													
☐ Black Vulture													
☐ Turkey Vulture	★												
☐ Osprey	★												
☐ Bald Eagle	★												
☐ Northern Harrier	★												
☐ Sharp-shinned Hawk	★												
☐ Cooper's Hawk	★												
☐ Northern Goshawk	★												
☐ Red-shouldered Hawk	★												
☐ Broad-winged Hawk	★												
☐ Red-tailed Hawk	★												
☐ Rough-legged Hawk													
☐ Golden Eagle													
☐ American Kestrel	★												
☐ Merlin													
☐ Peregrine Falcon	★												
☐ Gyrfalcon													
☐ Ring-necked Pheasant	★												
☐ Spruce Grouse	★												
☐ Ruffed Grouse	★												

✓	BREEDING?	January	February	March	April	May	June	July	August	September	October	November	December
☐ Wild Turkey	★												
☐ Northern Bobwhite	★												
☐ Yellow Rail													
☐ Clapper Rail													
☐ King Rail													
☐ Virginia Rail	★												
☐ Sora	★												
☐ Common Moorhen	★												
☐ American Coot													
☐ Sandhill Crane													
☐ Black-bellied Plover													
☐ American Golden-Plover													
☐ Semipalmated Plover													
☐ Piping Plover													
☐ Killdeer	★												
☐ American Oystercatcher													
☐ American Avocet													
☐ Greater Yellowlegs													
☐ Lesser Yellowlegs													
☐ Solitary Sandpiper													
☐ Willet	★												
☐ Spotted Sandpiper	★												
☐ Upland Sandpiper	★												
☐ Whimbrel													
☐ Hudsonian Godwit													
☐ Marbled Godwit													
☐ Ruddy Turnstone													
☐ Red Knot													

✔	BREEDING?	January	February	March	April	May	June	July	August	September	October	November	December
☐ Sanderling													
☐ Semipalmated Sandpiper													
☐ Western Sandpiper													
☐ Least Sandpiper													
☐ White-rumped Sandpiper													
☐ Baird's Sandpiper													
☐ Pectoral Sandpiper													
☐ Purple Sandpiper													
☐ Dunlin													
☐ Curlew Sandpiper													
☐ Stilt Sandpiper													
☐ Buff-breasted Sandpiper													
☐ Short-billed Dowitcher													
☐ Long-billed Dowitcher													
☐ Common Snipe	★												
☐ American Woodcock	★												
☐ Wilson's Phalarope													
☐ Red-necked Phalarope													
☐ Red Phalarope													
☐ Pomarine Jaeger													
☐ Parasitic Jaeger													
☐ Long-tailed Jaeger													
☐ Great Skua													
☐ Laughing Gull													
☐ Franklin's Gull													
☐ Little Gull													
☐ Common Black-headed Gull													
☐ Bonaparte's Gull													

✓	BREEDING?	January	February	March	April	May	June	July	August	September	October	November	December
☐ Ring-billed Gull	★												
☐ Herring Gull	★												
☐ Iceland Gull													
☐ Lesser Black-backed Gull													
☐ Glaucous Gull													
☐ Great Black-backed Gull	★												
☐ Black-legged Kittiwake													
☐ Sabine's Gull													
☐ Caspian Tern													
☐ Royal Tern													
☐ Sandwich Tern													
☐ Roseate Tern													
☐ Common Tern	★												
☐ Arctic Tern													
☐ Forster's Tern													
☐ Least Tern													
☐ Black Tern													
☐ Black Skimmer													
☐ Dovekie													
☐ Common Murre													
☐ Thick-billed Murre													
☐ Razorbill													
☐ Black Guillemot													
☐ Atlantic Puffin													
☐ Rock Dove	★												
☐ Mourning Dove	★												
☐ Black-billed Cuckoo	★												
☐ Yellow-billed Cuckoo	★												

✓	BREEDING?	January	February	March	April	May	June	July	August	September	October	November	December
☐ Barn Owl													
☐ Eastern Screech-Owl	★												
☐ Great Horned Owl	★												
☐ Snowy Owl													
☐ Northern Hawk Owl													
☐ Barred Owl	★												
☐ Great Gray Owl													
☐ Long-eared Owl	★												
☐ Short-eared Owl													
☐ Boreal Owl													
☐ Northern Saw-whet Owl	★												
☐ Common Nighthawk	★												
☐ Whip-poor-will	★												
☐ Chimney Swift	★												
☐ Ruby-throated Hummingbird	★												
☐ Rufous Hummingbird													
☐ Belted Kingfisher	★												
☐ Red-headed Woodpecker	★												
☐ Red-bellied Woodpecker													
☐ Yellow-bellied Sapsucker	★												
☐ Downy Woodpecker	★												
☐ Hairy Woodpecker	★												
☐ Three-toed Woodpecker	★												
☐ Black-backed Woodpecker	★												
☐ Northern Flicker	★												
☐ Pileated Woodpecker	★												
☐ Olive-sided Flycatcher	★												
☐ Eastern Wood-Pewee	★												

✓	BREEDING?	January	February	March	April	May	June	July	August	September	October	November	December
☐ Yellow-bellied Flycatcher	★												
☐ Acadian Flycatcher	★												
☐ Alder Flycatcher	★												
☐ Willow Flycatcher	★												
☐ Least Flycatcher	★												
☐ Eastern Phoebe	★												
☐ Great Crested Flycatcher	★												
☐ Western Kingbird													
☐ Eastern Kingbird	★												
☐ Horned Lark	★												
☐ Purple Martin	★												
☐ Tree Swallow	★												
☐ Nor. Rough-winged Swallow	★												
☐ Bank Swallow	★												
☐ Cliff Swallow	★												
☐ Barn Swallow	★												
☐ Gray Jay	★												
☐ Blue Jay	★												
☐ American Crow	★												
☐ Fish Crow													
☐ Common Raven	★												
☐ Black-capped Chickadee	★												
☐ Boreal Chickadee	★												
☐ Tufted Titmouse	★												
☐ Red-breasted Nuthatch	★												
☐ White-breasted Nuthatch	★												
☐ Brown Creeper	★												
☐ Carolina Wren	★												

✓	BREEDING?	January	February	March	April	May	June	July	August	September	October	November	December
☐ House Wren	★												
☐ Winter Wren	★												
☐ Sedge Wren	★												
☐ Marsh Wren	★												
☐ Golden-crowned Kinglet	★												
☐ Ruby-crowned Kinglet	★												
☐ Blue-gray Gnatcatcher	★												
☐ Northern Wheatear													
☐ Eastern Bluebird	★												
☐ Veery	★												
☐ Gray-cheeked Thrush													
☐ Bicknell's Thrush	★												
☐ Swainson's Thrush	★												
☐ Hermit Thrush	★												
☐ Wood Thrush	★												
☐ American Robin	★												
☐ Varied Thrush													
☐ Gray Catbird	★												
☐ Northern Mockingbird	★												
☐ Brown Thrasher	★												
☐ American Pipit	★												
☐ Bohemian Waxwing													
☐ Cedar Waxwing	★												
☐ Northern Shrike													
☐ Loggerhead Shrike													
☐ European Starling	★												
☐ White-eyed Vireo													
☐ Solitary Vireo	★												

✓	BREEDING?	January	February	March	April	May	June	July	August	September	October	November	December
☐ Yellow-throated Vireo	★												
☐ Warbling Vireo	★												
☐ Philadelphia Vireo	★												
☐ Red-eyed Vireo	★												
☐ Blue-winged Warbler	★												
☐ Golden-winged Warbler	★												
☐ Tennessee Warbler	★												
☐ Orange-crowned Warbler													
☐ Nashville Warbler	★												
☐ Northern Parula	★												
☐ Yellow Warbler	★												
☐ Chestnut-sided Warbler	★												
☐ Magnolia Warbler	★												
☐ Cape May Warbler	★												
☐ Black-throated Blue Warbler	★												
☐ Yellow-rumped Warbler	★												
☐ Black-throated Green Warbler	★												
☐ Blackburnian Warbler	★												
☐ Yellow-throated Warbler													
☐ Pine Warbler	★												
☐ Prairie Warbler	★												
☐ Palm Warbler	★												
☐ Bay-breasted Warbler	★												
☐ Blackpoll Warbler	★												
☐ Cerulean Warbler													
☐ Black-and-white Warbler	★												
☐ American Redstart	★												
☐ Prothonotary Warbler													

✓	BREEDING?	January	February	March	April	May	June	July	August	September	October	November	December
☐ Worm-eating Warbler													
☐ Ovenbird	★												
☐ Northern Waterthrush	★												
☐ Louisiana Waterthrush	★												
☐ Kentucky Warbler													
☐ Connecticut Warbler													
☐ Mourning Warbler	★												
☐ Common Yellowthroat	★												
☐ Hooded Warbler													
☐ Wilson's Warbler	★												
☐ Canada Warbler	★												
☐ Yellow-breasted Chat													
☐ Summer Tanager													
☐ Scarlet Tanager	★												
☐ Northern Cardinal	★												
☐ Rose-breasted Grosbeak	★												
☐ Blue Grosbeak													
☐ Indigo Bunting	★												
☐ Dickcissel													
☐ Rufous-sided Towhee	★												
☐ American Tree Sparrow													
☐ Chipping Sparrow	★												
☐ Clay-colored Sparrow													
☐ Field Sparrow	★												
☐ Vesper Sparrow	★												
☐ Lark Sparrow													
☐ Savannah Sparrow	★												
☐ Grasshopper Sparrow	★												

✓	BREEDING?	January	February	March	April	May	June	July	August	September	October	November	December
☐ Henslow's Sparrow													
☐ Salt-marsh Sharp-tailed Sparrow	★												
☐ Nelson's Sharp-tailed Sparrow													
☐ Seaside Sparrow	★												
☐ Fox Sparrow													
☐ Song Sparrow	★												
☐ Lincoln's Sparrow	★												
☐ Swamp Sparrow	★												
☐ White-throated Sparrow	★												
☐ White-crowned Sparrow													
☐ Harris's Sparrow													
☐ Dark-eyed Junco	★												
☐ Lapland Longspur													
☐ Snow Bunting													
☐ Bobolink	★												
☐ Red-winged Blackbird	★												
☐ Eastern Meadowlark	★												
☐ Yellow-headed Blackbird													
☐ Rusty Blackbird	★												
☐ Common Grackle	★												
☐ Brown-headed Cowbird	★												
☐ Orchard Oriole	★												
☐ Baltimore Oriole	★												
☐ Pine Grosbeak	★												
☐ Purple Finch	★												
☐ House Finch	★												
☐ Red Crossbill	★												
☐ White-winged Crossbill	★												

✓	BREEDING?	January	February	March	April	May	June	July	August	September	October	November	December
☐ Common Redpoll													
☐ Hoary Redpoll													
☐ Pine Siskin	★												
☐ American Goldfinch	★												
☐ Evening Grosbeak	★												
☐ House Sparrow	★												

Appendix:

OTHER ANIMALS OF NEW HAMPSHIRE

MAMMALS

Virginia Opossum *(Didelphis marsupialis)*
Masked Shrew *(Sorex cinereus)*
Smoky Shrew *(Sorex fumeus)*
Long-tailed Shrew *(Sorex dispar)*
Northern Water-Shrew *(Sorex palustris)*
Pygmy Shrew *(Microsorex hoyi)*
Short-tailed Shrew *(Blarina brevicauda)*
Star-nosed Mole *(Condylura cristata)*
Hairy-tailed Mole *(Parascalops breweri)*
Keen's Myotis *(Myotis keeni)*
Little Brown Myotis *(Myotis lucifugus)*
Small-footed Myotis *(Myotis subulatus)*
Eastern Pipistrelle *(Pipistrellus subflavus)*
Silver-haired Bat *(Lasionycteris noctivagans)*
Big Brown Bat *(Eptesicus fuscus)*
Red Bat *(Lasiurus borealis)*
Hoary Bat *(Lasiurus cinereus)*
Black Bear *(Ursus americanus)*
Raccoon *(Procyon lotor)*
Pine Marten *(Martes americana)*
Fisher *(Martes pennanti)*
Shorttail Weasel *(Mustela erminea)*
Longtail Weasel *(Mustela frenata)*
Mink *(Mustela vison)*
River Otter *(Lutra canadensis)*
Striped Skunk *(Mephitis mephitis)*
Coyote *(Canis latrans)*
Red Fox *(Vulpes fulva)*
Gray Fox *(Urocyon cinereoargenteus)*
Lynx *(Lynx canadensis)*
Bobcat *(Lynx rufus)*
Harbor Seal *(Phoca vitulina)*
Woodchuck *(Marmota monax)*
Eastern Chipmunk *(Tamias striatus)*
Eastern Gray Squirrel *(Sciurus carolinensis)*
Red Squirrel *(Tamiasciurus hudsonicus)*
Southern Flying-Squirrel *(Glaucomys volans)*

Northern Flying-Squirrel *(Glaucomys sabrinus)*
Beaver *(Castor canadensis)*
Deer Mouse *(Peromyscus maniculatus)*
White-footed Mouse *(Peromyscus leucopus)*
Northern Bog-Lemming *(Synaptomys borealis)*
Southern Bog-Lemming *(Synaptomys cooperi)*
Boreal Redback Vole *(Clethrionomys gapperi)*
Meadow Vole *(Microtus pennsylvanicus)*
Yellownose Vole *(Microtus chrotorrhinus)*
Pine Vole *(Pitymus pinetorum)*
Muskrat *(Ondatra zibethica)*
Norway Rat *(Rattus norvegicus)*
House Mouse *(Mus musculus)*
Meadow Jumping-Mouse *(Zapus hudsonius)*
Woodland Jumping-Mouse *(Napaeozapus insignis)*
Porcupine *(Erethizon dorsatum)*
Snowshoe Hare *(Lepus americanus)*
Eastern Cottontail *(Sylvilagus floridanus)*
New England Cottontail *(Sylvilagus transitionalis)*
White-tailed Deer *(Odocoileus virginianus)*
Moose *(Alces alces)*
Common Dolphin *(Delphinus delphis)*
Atlantic White-sided Dolphin *(Lagenorhynchus acutus)*
Pilot Whale *(Globicephala melaena)*
Harbor Porpoise *(Phocoena phocoena)*
Finback Whale *(Balaenoptera physalus)*
Minke Whale *(Balaenoptera acutorostrata)*
Blue Whale *(Balaenoptera musculus)*
Humpback Whale *(Megaptera novaeangliae)*
Northern Right Whale *(Balaena glacialis)*

REPTILES

Black Racer *(Coluber constrictor constrictor)*
Timber Rattlesnake *(Crotalus horridus horridus)*
Eastern Garter Snake *(Thamnophis sirtalis sirtalis)*
Eastern Ribbon Snake *(Thamnophis sauritus sauritus)*
Eastern Hognose Snake *(Heterodon platyrhinos)*
Eastern Milk Snake *(Lampropeltis triangulum triangulum)*
Smooth Green Snake *(Opheodrys vernalis)*
Northern Brown Snake *(Storeria dekayi dekayi)*
Red-bellied Snake *(Storeria occipitomaculata)*
Northern Ringneck Snake *(Diadophis punctatus edwardsi)*
Northern Water Snake *(Nerodia sipedon sipedon)*
Blanding's Turtle *(Emydoidea blandingi)*
Common Musk (Stinkpot) Turtle *(Sternotherus odoratus)*
Eastern Box Turtle *(Terrapene carolina carolina)*
Eastern Painted Turtle *(Chrysemys picta picta)*
Midland Painted Turtle *(Chrysemys picta marginata)*
Snapping Turtle *(Chelydra serpentina)*

Spotted Turtle *(Clemmys guttata)*
Wood Turtle *(Clemmys insculpta)*

AMPHIBIANS

Bullfrog *(Rana catesbeiana)*
Green Frog *(Rana clamitans melanota)*
Mink Frog *(Rana septentrionalis)*
Northern Leopard Frog *(Rana pipiens)*
Pickerel Frog *(Rana palustris)*
Wood Frog *(Rana sylvatica)*
Mudpuppy *(Necturus maculosus)*
Red-spotted Newt *(Notophthalmus viridescens viridescens)*
Spring Peeper *(Hyla [Pseudacris]crucifer)*
Gray Treefrog *(Hyla versicolor)*
Blue-spotted Salamander *(Ambystoma laterale)*
Four-toed Salamander *(Hemidactylium scutatum)*
Jefferson Salamander *(Ambystoma jeffersonianum)*
Marbled Salamander *(Ambystoma opacum)*
Northern Dusky Salamander *(Desmognathus fuscus fuscus)*
Spring Salamander *(Gyrinophilus porphyriticus)*
Two-lined Salamander *(Eurycea bislineata bislineata)*
Red-backed Salamander *(Plethodon cinereus cinereus)*
Slimy Salamander *(Plethodon glutinosus glutinosus)*
Spotted Salamander *(Ambystoma maculatum)*
American Toad *(Bufo americanus)*
Fowler's Toad *(Bufo woodhousei fowleri)*

BUTTERFLIES

Swallowtails *Papilionidae*
Black Swallowtail *(Papilio polyxenes)*
Eastern Tiger Swallowtail *(Papilio glaucus)*
Canadian Tiger Swallowtail *(Papilio canadensis)*
Spicebush Swallowtail *(Papilio troilus)*
Whites and Sulphurs *Pieridae*
Mustard (or Veined) White *(Pieris napi)*
West Virginia White *(Pieris virginiensis)*
Cabbage White *(Pieris rapae)*
Clouded Sulphur *(Colias philodice)*
Orange Sulphur *(Colias eurytheme)*
Pink-edged Sulphur *(Colias interior)*
Little Yellow *(Eurema lisa)*
Gossamer Wings *Lycaenidae*
Harvester *(Feniseca tarquinius)*
American Copper *(Lycaena phlaeas)*
Bronze Copper *(Lycaena hyllus)*
Bog Copper *(Lycaena epixanthe)*
Coral Hairstreak *(Satyrium titus)*

Edwards's Hairstreak *(Satyrium edwardsii)*
Banded Hairstreak *(Satyrium calanus)*
Hickory Hairstreak *(Satyrium caryaevorum)*
Striped Hairstreak *(Saryrium liparops)*
Juniper Hairstreak *(Mitoura grynea)*
Brown Elfin *(Callophrys augustinus)*
Hoary Elfin *(Callophrys polia)*
Frosted Elfin *(Callophrys irus)*
Henry's Elfin *(Callophrys henrici)*
Bog Elfin *(Callophrys lanoraieensis)*
Eastern Pine Elfin *(Callophrys niphon)*
Early Hairstreak *(Erora laetus)*
Gray Hairstreak *(Strymon melinus)*
Eastern Tailed Blue *(Everes comyntas)*
Spring Azure *(Celastrina argiolus)*
Brushfoots *Nymphalidae*
Great Spangled Fritillary *(Speyeria cybele)*
Aphrodite Fritillary *(Speyeria aphrodite)*
Atlantis Fritillary *(Speyeria atlantis)*
Sliver-bordered Fritillary *(Boloria selene)*
Meadow Fritillary *(Boloria bellona)*
Titania Fritillary *(Boloria titania)*
Silvery Checkerspot *(Chlosyne nycteis)*
Harris's Checkerspot *(Chlosyne harrisii)*
Pearl Crescent *(Phyciodes tharos)*
Northern Crescent *(Phyciodes selenis)*
Baltimore *(Euphydryas phaeton)*
Question Mark *(Polygonia interrogationis)*
Eastern Comma *(Polygonia comma)*
Satyr Comma *(Polygonia satyrus)*
Green Comma *(Polygonia faunus)*
Hoary Comma *(Polygonia gracilis)*
Gray Comma *(Polygonia progne)*
Compton Tortoiseshell *(Nymphalis vau-album)*
Mourning Cloak *(Nymphalis antiopa)*
Milbert's Tortoiseshell *(Nymphalis milberti)*
Red Admiral *(Vanessa atalanta)*
American Lady *(Vanessa virginiensis)*
Painted Lady *(Vanessa cardui)*
Common Buckeye *(Junonia coenia)*
Red-spotted Purple *(Limenitis arthemis astyanax)*
White Admiral (or Banded Purple) *(Limenitis arthemis arthemis)*
Viceroy *(Limenitis archippus)*
Northern Pearly Eye *(Enodia anthedon)*
Eyed Brown *(Satyrodes eurydice)*
Appalachian Brown *(Satyrodes appalachia)*
Little Wood Satyr *(Megisto cymela)*
Common Ringlet *(Coenonympha tullia)*
Common Wood Nymph *(Cercyonis pegala)*
Jutta Arctic *(Oeneis jutta)*
Melissa Arctic *(Oeneis melissa)*
Polixenes Arctic *(Oeneis polixenes)*

Monarch *(Danaus plexippus)*
Skippers   Hesperiidae
Silver-spotted Skipper *(Epargyreus clarus)*
Northern Cloudywing *(Thorybes pylades)*
Dreamy Duskywing *(Erynnis icelus)*
Sleepy Duskywing *(Erynnis brizo)*
Juvenal's Duskywing *(Erynnis juvenalis)*
Horace's Duskywing *(Erynnis horatius)*
Mottled Duskywing *(Erynnis martialis)*
Columbine Duskywing *(Erynnis lucilius)*
Wild-Indigo Duskywing *(Erynnis baptisiae)*
Persius Duskywing *(Erynnis persius)*
Common Sootywing *(Pholisora catullus)*
Arctic Skipper *(Carterocephalus palaemon)*
Least Skipper *(Ancyloxpha numitor)*
European Skipper *(Thymelicus lineola)*
Common Branded Skipper *(Hespena comma)*
Leonard's Skipper *(Hespena leonardus)*
Cobweb Skipper *(Hespena metea)*
Indian Skipper *(Hespena sassacus)*
Peck's Skipper *(Polites peckius)*
Tawny-edged Skipper *(Polites themistocles)*
Crossline Skipper *(Polites origenes)*
Long Dash *(Polites mystic)*
Northern Broken Dash *(Wallengrenia egeremet)*
Little Glassywing *(Pompeius verna)*
Sachem *(Atalopdes campestris)*
Delaware Skipper *(Atrytone logan)*
Hobomok Skipper *(Poanes hobomok)*
Two-spotted Skipper *(Euphyes bimacula)*
Dun Skipper *(Euphyes vestris)*
Dusted Skipper *(Atrytonopsis hianna)*
Pepper-and-salt Skipper *(Amblyscirtes hegon)*
Common Roadside Skipper *(Amblyscirtes vialis)*

REFERENCES

Allen, Glover M. 1903. *A List of the Birds of New Hampshire.* Manchester Institute of Arts and Sciences.

The Appalachian Mountain Club. 1992. *The AMC White Mountain Guide,* twenty-fifth edition.

Audubon Society of New Hampshire. *New Hampshire Bird Records.*

Beecher, Ned. 1989. *Outdoor Explorations in Mt. Washington Valley.* Tin Mountain Conservation Center.

Bird Observer of Eastern Massachusetts, Inc. *Bird Observer.*

Burt, William Henry, and Richard Philip Grossenheider. 1964. *A Field Guide to the Mammals.* Houghton Mifflin Co., Boston.

Brewster, William. 1924-1938. *The Birds of the Lake Umbagog Region of Maine.* Bulletin of the Museum of Comparative Zoology.

Casanave, S. 1994. *Natural Wonders of New Hampshire.* Country Roads Press, Castine, Maine.

Collins, Henry Hill, Jr., et al. 1981. *Complete Field Guide to North American Wildlife. Eastern Edition.* Harper & Row, New York.

Conant, Roger. 1958 and newer editions. *A Field Guide to the Reptiles and Amphibians of Eastern North America.* Houghton Mifflin Co., Boston.

Dearborn, Ned. 1898. *A Preliminary List of the Birds of Belknap and Merrimack Counties, NH, with notes.* M.S. Thesis, N.H. College of Agriculture and Mechanic Arts.

Dearborn, Ned. 1903. *The Birds of Durham and Vicinity.* Doctoral Thesis, N.H. College of Agriculture and Mechanic Arts.

Delorey, Alan. 1992. "The Power-line Right-of-way: An Unexpected Place to Find Many Nesting Birds". *Birding.* 24(6):365-367.

Delorey, Alan. 1991. "Our 100th Backyard Species". *Bird Watcher's Digest.* 13(6):88-91.

DeLorme Mapping Company. 1988. *The New Hampshire Atlas and Gazetteer.*

Elkins, Kimball C. 1982. *A Checklist of the Birds of New Hampshire.* Audubon Society of New Hampshire.

Foss, Carol R. (ed.) 1995. *Atlas of Breeding Birds of New Hampshire.* Audubon Society of New Hampshire.

Glassberg, Jeffrey. 1993. *Butterflies Through Binoculars*. Oxford University Press, New York.

Holland, W. J. 1898, 1931, and 1951. *The Butterfly Book*. Doubleday & Co., New York.

Kastner, Joseph. 1986. *A World of Watchers*. Alfred A. Knopf.

Klots, Alexander B. 1951 and newer editions. *A Field Guide to the Butterflies of North America, East of the Great Plains*. Houghton Mifflin Co., Boston.

Kricher, John C. 1988. *A Field Guide to Eastern Forests*. Houghton Mifflin Co., Boston.

Merrill, Pauline S. "History of Audubon Society of New Hampshire". *New Hampshire Audubon Quarterly*, October 1961 and April 1962.

National Geographic Society. 1987. *Birds of North America*, second edition.

Pettingill, Olin Sewall, Jr. 1977. *A Guide to Bird Finding East of the Mississippi*, second edition. Oxford University Press, New York.

Pettingill, Olin Sewall Jr. 1965. Second edition 1974. *The Bird Watcher's America*. Apollo Editions.

Richards, Tudor. 1967. *Animal Life in the White Mountains Region*. New Hampshire Audubon Brief Guide to the Natural History of the White Mountains.

Steele, Frederic L. 1982. *At Timberline: A Nature Guide to the Mountains of the Northeast*. Appalachian Mountain Club, Boston.

Terres, John K. 1980. *The Audubon Society Encyclopedia of North American Birds*. Alfred A. Knopf, Inc.

Walton, Richard K. 1988. *Bird Finding in New England*. Godine.

White, F.B. 1924. *A Preliminary List of Birds of Concord, New Hampshire*. The Rumford Press, Concord, NH.

Wright, Horace W. 1911. *The Birds of the Jefferson Region*. Manchester Institute of Arts and Sciences.

OTHER BIRDFINDING GUIDES
IN ABA/LANE SERIES

Birdfinder: A Birder's Guide to Planning North American Trips
by Jerry A. Cooper
1995, $17.95

A Birder's Guide to Southeastern Arizona
by Richard Cachor Taylor
1995, $16.95

A Birder's Guide to Arkansas
by Mel White
1995, $16.95

A Birder's Guide to Eastern Massachusetts
by Bird Observer
1994, $16.95

A Birder's Guide to Churchill (Manitoba)
by Bonnie Chartier
1993, $14.95

A Birder's Guide to Wyoming
by Oliver K. Scott
1993, $16.95

A Birder's Guide to the Texas Coast
by Harold R. Holt
1993, $14.95

A Birder's Guide to the Rio Grande Valley of Texas
by Harold R. Holt
1992, $16.95

A Birder's Guide to Southern California
by Harold R. Holt
1990, $14.95

A Birder's Guide to Florida
under revision

A Birder's Guide to Colorado
under revision

ABA

The Organization Devoted to North American Birders

ABA is *the* organization of North American birders, and its mission is to bring all the excitement, challenge, and wonder of birding to you. As an ABA member you will get the information you need to increase your birding skills so that you can make the most of your time in the field.

Each year members receive six issues of ABA's award-winning magazine, *Birding*, and twelve issues of *Winging It*, a monthly newsletter. ABA's periodicals put you in touch with the birding scene across the continent. ABA conducts regular conferences and biennial conventions in the continent's best birding areas, publishes a yearly *Membership Directory/Yellow Pages* to help you keep in touch, offers discount prices for bird books, optical gear, and other birding equipment through ABA Sales, and compiles an annual *Directory of Volunteer Opportunities* for members. The organization's *ABA/Lane Birdfinding Guides* set the standard for accuracy and excellence.

ABA is engaged in bird conservation through such activities as Partners in Flight and the American Bird Conservancy. ABA encourages birding among young people through youth birding camps and other activities, and publishes *A Bird's-Eye View*, a quarterly newsletter by and for its younger members. The organization promotes ethical birding practices. In short, the American Birding Association works to ensure that birds and birding have the healthy future they deserve.

"ABA is the best value in the birding community today."
Roger Tory Peterson

The American Birding Association gives active birders what they want. Consider joining today. You will find a membership application on the other side of this page.

American Birding Association
P.O. Box 6599
Colorado Springs, Colorado 80934

AMERICAN BIRDING ASSOCIATION
Membership Application

The American Birding Association is *the* organization of North American birders dedicated to being the main source for up-to-date information on bird identification, birdfinding, and bird conservation. The ABA gives active birders what they want.

All memberships include six issues of **Birding** magazine, monthly issues of **Winging It,** ABA's newsletter, member discounts offered by ABA Sales, and full rights of participation in all ABA activities.

Membership classes and dues:

❏ Individual - US	$36/yr	❏ Family - US	$43/yr
❏ Individual - Canada	$45/yr*	❏ Family - Canada	$52/yr*
❏ Individual - Int'l	$45/yr	❏ Family - Int'l	$52/yr
❏ Century Club	$100/yr	❏ Life Membership	$1,200

*All membership dues include $27 for **Birding** magazine and $9 for **Winging It** newsletter;*
* = includes GST

Application Type ❏ New Membership ❏ Renewal

Member Information

Name _____

Address _____

_____

_____

Phone _____

Payment Information

❏ Check or Money Order enclosed (US funds only)

❏ Charge to VISA / MasterCard (circle one)

Account Number _____

Exp Date _____ Signature _____

Sent this completed form with payment to: **ABA Membership**
PO Box 6599
Colorado Springs, CO 80934

NH 1/96

NOTES

NOTES

Nomenclature Changes

The bird names used in this book basically follow those of the American Ornithologists' Union (AOU) and the American Birding Association (ABA). Below are also some names which differ from those used in older field guides, or which yet to appear in even the most recent field guides.

Names Used in this Book	Former Name or Derivation
Green Heron	Green-backed Heron
Tundra Swan	Whistling Swan
Common Moorhen	Common Gallinule
American Golden-Plover	split from Lesser Golden-Plover
Bicknell's Thrush	split from Gray-cheeked Thrush
American Pipit	Water Pipit
Salt-marsh Sharp-tailed Sparrow	split from Sharp-tailed Sparrow
Nelson's Sharp-tailed Sparrow	split from Sharp-tailed Sparrow
Baltimore Oriole	split from Northern Oriole

INDEX

A

Adams Point 40-41
Airport Marsh 139
Akers Pond 172

Androscoggin State Wayside Picnic Area 172
Annett State Park 105
Appalachian Mountain Club (AMC) 15, 115
Appalachian Trail 135
Audubon Society of New Hampshire 3, 21, 81
Auk
  Great 2
Avocet
  American 26, 191

B

Back Lake 157, 159
Bartlett 141
Bear Brook Pond 174
Berlin 171
Bethlehem 135
Big Brook Bog 164
Bittern
  American 26, 70, 91, 93-94, 123, 129, 131, 139, 167, 171, 188
  Least 26-27, 35, 49, 94, 188
Blackbird
  Red-winged 53, 55, 61, 64, 66, 69, 76, 81, 90, 129-131, 180, 199
  Rusty 6, 15, 64, 139, 141, 143, 160, 165, 167-168, 199
  Yellow-headed 199
Blackwater Reservoir 97
Bluebird
  Eastern 41, 49, 83, 196
Bobolink 2, 41, 49, 77, 84, 139, 158, 199
Bobwhite
  Northern 2, 5, 75, 78, 139, 191
Bog Pond 129
Boundary Pond 166